REREADING THE *Sophists*

CLASSICAL RHETORIC

REFIGURED

Susan C. Jarratt

Southern Illinois University Press

Carbondale and Edwardsville

Library of Congress Cataloging-in-Publication Data
Jarratt, Susan C.
     Rereading the sophists: classical rhetoric refigured / Susan C.
Jarratt.
       p.   cm.
     Includes bibliographical references and index.
       1. Rhetoric, Ancient.   2. Sophists (Greek philosophy)   3.
Feminist criticism.   I. Title.
     PA3265.J37   1991   90-47156
     808'.00938—dc20   CIP
     ISBN 0-8093-1616-1

Earlier versions of chapter 1 were published in *Rhetoric Review* 6
(1987) and *PRE/TEXT* 8 (1987). A portion of chapter 2 appeared in
Susan C. Jarratt, "The Role of the Sophists in Histories of
Consciousness," *Philosophy and Rhetoric* vol. 23, no. 2, 1990: 85–95.
Copyright 1990 by the Pennsylvania State University. Reproduced
by permission of the publisher. Chapter 3 appeared in a different
form in *Hypatia: A Journal of Feminist Philosophy* (Winter 1990) and
in *Discurrendo* (Winter 1990).

Frontispiece: Greek grave *stele,* sixth century B.C. (Louvre, Paris).
Photograph by Peter W. Rose.

The paper used in this publication meets the minimum
requirements of American National Standard for Information
Sciences—Permanence of Paper for Printed Library Materials,
ANSI Z39.48-1984.

To my mother
Edyce Wheeler Funderburgh
and my daughter
Jessica Lee Jarratt

Every advance in
epistemology and moral knowledge
has reinstated the Sophists

Friedrich Nietzsche, *Will to Power*

CONTENTS

PREFACE

I N THE frontispiece illustration, you see a woman taking something out of a box. The notes describing this sixth-century B.C. grave marker tell us that we do not know what it is she handles. It could be a text, thus making this artifact valuable evidence for women's early literacy. Or, more likely, the description reads, she holds a cosmetics box. This interpretation reaffirms the persistent view of women as superficial and deceptive: those who cover up the true and natural with a beautiful but artificial surface, making it seem to be something other than it really is.

I chose this image to grace my work on the sophists because it offers a visual analog for my project. The woman historian uncovers something—the reader is not sure what—either a text to be read and considered seriously, or else materials for painting a face on something. If I am preparing to "make something up," then who is more in need of embellishment, some might say, than the first sophists: arch-deceptors, enemies of Truth, manipulators of language? If I prepare to read a text, how fitting that the image is blurred, for remains of the sophists are fragmented and doubtful. Like the sophists, given two choices, I take both, weighing the one against the other. This study is both a serious attempt to reconsider the sophists and a chance to dress them up, to make the worse case better. With my ancient sister on the cover, Pandora-like, I open the box and hold my breath, waiting to see what comes out.

Opening the box has taken quite a long time, and the longer I look, the more I see. The reader can trace those changes through the chapters. I begin with an impulse, a wish, an intuition—a desire for a different kind of history. As a student of classical rhetoric, I was uneasy with the received version of its beginnings in Greece; I was drawn to the sophists by the vituperation poured on them by their successors. Thus, my first relation to the sophists was as rediscoverer and defender. Asking why the sophists had been so treated, my search for their history became an inquiry into historiography. As I encountered political issues in the field of rhetoric and composition— questions about how history should be written, about orality and literacy, about feminism and critical pedagogy—the sophists provided provocative answers. The most exciting moment in this work was the connection with feminism, and I now see the whole project, as the frontispiece suggests, in terms of gendered historiography—a woman's search for a different kind of history.

During the work of this book, I have enjoyed the help of many— scholars, friends, and family. It began in graduate school with my dissertation. Though they would recognize little of that early effort in this text, John Farrell, James Kinneavy, Greg Myers, and Patricia Kruppa helped to launch the project. A strong network of compatriots in rhetoric has provided encouragement and support from the beginning of my public pronouncements on the sophists. Jim Berlin, Patricia Bizzell, Sharon Crowley, Beth Daniell, Richard Enos, Patricia Harkin, Takis Poulakos, John Schilb, Jan Swearingen, Victor Vitanza, and Lynn Worsham have been steady supporters, good readers, and lively interlocutors in dozens of conversations about the history of rhetoric. I am grateful to Don Bialostowski, Barbara Biesecker, Theresa Enos, Michael Halloran, Henry Johnstone, and Chuck Schuster for providing forums for discussion of the sophists. Jerry Murphy, Richard Enos, and Jasper Neel provided generous and insightful readings of the manuscript. Though it may not have ended up as any one of them would have wished, I have learned much from their responses. I wish to thank Kenney Withers, director of Southern Illinois University Press, for his enthusiastic support and fine editorial guidance. Susan Wilson and George Nicholas were most helpful in the copyediting of the manuscript.

Colleagues and students at Miami University have sustained this project with many kinds of support. Dale Bauer has been a stalwart friend, a critical reader, and co-creator of feminist sophistics. I thank her and Kristina Straub for bringing me to feminism and modeling committed feminist activism in the academy. Linda Singer shared her rare gifts of personal warmth, irrepressible wit, and finely honed critical insight. Jim Sosnoski offered friendship and support, especially during my first year. Steve Nimis generously included me in several Greek classes. Graduate students in classical rhetoric have helped me work through historiographical questions in rhetoric and problems with the reception of the sophists: I appreciate especially the help of Maggy Lindgren, Rory Ong, Nedra Reynolds, Joy Rouse, and Marian Sciachitano. I am grateful to the English Department at Miami University for a semester off in the fall of 1988 during which the parts of the book came together. My heaviest and lightest debt is to Peter Rose, a steadfast comrade, who has generously shared his rich knowledge of Greek literature and history, his passionate political commitments, and his nourishing companionship with me for the most formative years of this project.

Friends and family have had less to do with the book itself but everything to do with the well-being of its author during its composition. Gina Palmer and David Bates have been the truest of friends—intellectual and moral touchstones since graduate school. Following Gorgias, they always cure my seriousness with laughter. To Nancy and Pat Jarratt I owe many thanks; their generous support has kept my academic enterprises afloat for years. If my father were still alive, I would thank him for helping me through the many years of school he never had. The dedication expresses my deepest obligation: to those women whose sacrifices for me and faith in me have, in the most heartfelt way, made my work possible.

And it is time to change.
To invent the other history . . .

Hélène Cixous, *The Newly Born Woman*

Introduction: Redefining Classical Rhetoric

THE NEWLY emergent field of rhetoric and composition has begun to discover its history in a classical tradition. But so far, accounts of that tradition have had more to say about Aristotle, Cicero, and Quintilian than the supposed inventors of the art: the first sophists.[1] The aim of this book is to investigate the reasons why the sophists have only lately begun to enter the conversation about histories of rhetoric and to make a case for giving them a more prominent role in those histories. Such a defense might begin simply on the grounds that the first sophists were the first to offer systematic instruction in the arts of speaking and writing in the West. The emergence of democracy in fifth-century B.C. Athens, demanding broader participation in government and legal affairs, created the need for a kind of secondary education designed to prepare young men for public life in the *polis* (Kerferd 15; Marrou 47–48; Kennedy, *Rhetoric* 18–19). The first or elder sophists—Protagoras of Abdera, Gorgias of Leontini, Prodicus, Hippias, and others—filled that need.[2] These well-traveled, charismatic teachers offered to those who could pay their substantial fees an intense and personal training in the *techne* (art) of rhetoric, i.e., speaking persuasively in the public assembly and before judges. This skill was the most important measure of success in public life in fifth-century Athens (Kerferd 17; Guthrie, *Sophists* 44). Their effectiveness in teaching this *techne* derived in part from their experiences of different cultures; they believed and taught that notions of "truth" had to be adjusted to fit the ways of a particular audience in a certain time and with a certain set of beliefs and laws. Thus they advanced concepts of *kairos* (timeliness) and *to prepon* (fitness).

This picture of the sophists, however, has often (lead) to the conclusion that they are to be understood in merely pragmatic terms, discounting the "philosophic" seriousness of their project. Historically, the reduction of the sophistic project to the exercise of a particular style (Murphy, *History* 8), to an exhibition of personal power by the orator (Kennedy, *Rhetoric* 16–17, 31 passim), or at worst to the amoral manipulation of an audience (Sidgwick) indicates the powerful influence on histories of rhetoric by Plato and Aristotle. Plato's denigration of rhetoric as akin to cooking and cosmetics in *Gorgias*, for example, is too well known to need much rehearsal. Despite the fact that Socrates does give rhetoric a role in *Phaedrus*, the rhetoric he describes is chastened in service of "truth" already discovered through dialectic. Once a metaphysical epistemology is put in place dividing being from seeming, substance from appearance, wisdom from eloquence, then a reductive picture of "rhetoric" can be created, conveniently combining all the negative poles in each opposition, displacing them in favor of "philosophy" (*Phaedrus* ¶260–262).[3] In Aristotle's world as well, realms of knowledge are divided; "rhetoric" is a faculty (a process or method) functioning only in fields of probable knowledge, i.e., politics, ethics, and law (*Rhetoric* I. iv. 5). He specifies that knowledge of the natural world or of metaphysics— indeed of any specific "science"—is out of the scope of rhetoric's powers (I. v. 6–7). Studies of first causes of objects in the world require a different process of discovery and logical framework for articulation, namely induction and syllogism. Another Aristotelian division brackets literature, apart from both probable and certain knowledge, as a kind of "making" in imitation of life (*Poetics* I. i. 15). Not only does Aristotle divide knowledge, he ranks it. Rhetoric as a practical art is subordinate to the search for universals conducted by "speculative" sciences (*Metaphysics* VI. i. 11). Productive arts as well, like literature, must be directed by "true reason" (*Nicomachean Ethics* VI. 4). Though practical wisdom plays an important role in the life of the good citizen for Aristotle, it is dependent on and ultimately inferior to "theoretical wisdom," i.e., the knowledge of permanent truths derived through induction and syllogistic logic (*Nicomachean Ethics* VI. 1–12, especially 7.20 and 12.30–35; *Metaphysics* II. 1. 6–7).

Despite the subordinate role Aristotle assigns rhetoric in his system of thought, his voice has dominated the current revival of rhetoric as a historical study. An obvious reason is that his *Rhetoric* is the most complete ancient treatment of the subject. Two ground-breaking works, Corbett's *Classical Rhetoric for the Modern Student* (1963) and Kinneavy's *Theory of Discourse* (1971), rely directly on Aristotle in making available for the first time to twentieth-century composition teachers a fully developed history and a theory of rhetoric.[4] Even when Aristotle is not the center of a work, the application of tools such as the tripartite division of persuasive techniques (*logos, ethos,* and *pathos*) or the communication triangle index his influence.[5] Perspectives on the field seem to have broadened since the pioneering efforts of Corbett and Kinneavy. George A. Kennedy's early history, for example, *The Art of Persuasion in Greece,* presented a very brief and negative view of the sophists; whereas his later *Classical Rhetoric and Its Christian and Secular Tradition from Ancient to Modern Times* provides a more extensive and judicious treatment. But, in fact, Kennedy's whole organizational scheme derives from Aristotle's communication model (*Rhetoric* 16), providing him with a privileged category called "philosophical rhetoric" from which the sophists are excluded.[6]

Aristotle, indeed, offers a rich and complicated view of rhetoric well worth investigating.[7] But a more crucial issue than the mere presence or absence of a particular classical figure is the often unspoken acceptance of foundational features of Aristotelian thought on which current histories sometimes rest. Particular discourses—rhetorical or other—are always located within a knowledge structure: i.e., an *episteme* (Foucault, *Order* xx–xxii) or noetic field (Berlin, *Writing* 2). A historian, then, who uses Aristotle uncritically as a point of departure may be in danger of reinscribing the epistemic field within which his rhetoric dwelt.[8] The purpose of rereading the first sophists for rhetoric and composition studies today is to bring to light that Aristotelian orientation and offer an alternative. In reconstructing the sophists, the task lies in bringing to awareness the screen through which they are inevitably filtered for us by our location on the other side of Aristotle, and then in re-seeing them, as far as is possible, within their own fifth-century intellectual, political, and artistic milieu. The results will enrich our historical backgrounds and may cast new light on contemporary concerns in the field of rhetoric and composition.

The sophists, taken as an alternative warrant for the conceptualization and practice of rhetoric, offer quite a different epistemic field from that mapped by Aristotle. Rejecting traditional religion as an explanation for natural phenomena, they evinced a special interest in human perceptions as the only source of knowledge in all fields, including nature, and emphasized the significance of language in constructing that knowledge. In fact, their thought is considered by some crucial in the epistemic shift called the Greek enlightenment.[9] But the sophists' role in that revolution is usually eclipsed in histories of rhetoric because of the dearth of textual remains, Plato's censure and distortion (Havelock, *Temper*), and the seductive presence of Aristotle's full systematization of all these realms (*Rhetoric, Organon, Physics, Metaphysics, Politics, Nicomachean Ethics*). Even to adopt the concept of "epistemic shift" means renouncing foundational features of Aristotelian thought. Though Aristotle's texts on ethics and politics indicate a sensitivity to the complexities of human action in those fields, this understanding must be placed against the background of his fixed vision of *episteme*. A revised view would call into question the hierarchy of such categories and ask whether and how the sophists answer the questions treated by "philosophy": what are the origins of life and thought, how can knowledge be defined, and what is "reality." The crucial difference from Plato and Aristotle is that the sophists make possible an additional question—a question virtually unavoidable in the current critical climate: how does language create different answers to those questions at different moments in history?

Lumping together Plato and Aristotle, as I do here, requires more explanation than a footnote. The texts of these two philosophers are, of course, quite distinct and much more complex than this study will reveal. They are beginning to come under critical analysis within the field of rhetoric and composition.[10] But despite these complexities, the two fourth-century philosophers have together grounded a tradition which has suppressed the positions the sophists advocated— the primacy of human knowledge, possibilities for non-rational and

emotional responses to the whole range of discourse types, a fundamental understanding of knowledge and values as historically contingent, a recognition of all discourse as "rhetorical," an integral relationship between theory, practice and the political sphere (IJsseling).[11] It
may be more useful to refer to "Platonism" and "Aristotelianism,"
rather than the proper names themselves, as the tendencies I aim to
counter by rereading the sophists.[12]

The pioneering histories of rhetoric produced early in the current
revival (Kennedy, Corbett, and Kinneavy) have served virtually to
bring into existence for a twentieth-century audience authors and
texts ignored under the philosophic tradition. The task at hand now
is to examine more closely the method of reading we bring to those
texts and, more broadly, to the whole discursive field within which
they take their places. The result will be different readings of canonical
texts, as well as the identification of new significant sites of "rhetoric"
in its more comprehensive sophistic definition. In a contemporary
critical context, all kinds of knowing and performing have become
subject to analysis under the wider heading of discursive practice.
Nietzsche sought to explode the "scientific" basis of philosophy and
natural law ("Truth and Lies"). Foucault investigated the rules by
which disciplinary boundaries establish themselves (*Archaeology*).
Derrida exposed the binary system of signification underlying "meaning" in Western philosophy (B. Johnson viii–x). Following Nietzsche, White argued for the literary nature of any historical narrative
("Fictions," *Metahistory*). Questioning an Aristotelian orientation for
describing the history of rhetoric and seeking to provide an alternative
is, in part, an attempt to take into account those changes, to recreate
the classical roots of rhetoric in their light.

One possible course for the contemporary rhetorician would be
to jettison those classical origins as unassimilable to a contemporary
context (Knoblauch and Brannon; S. Miller). But I propose that a
more comprehensive view of "the tradition" will provide rich ante-
cedents for later rhetorical developments. In the century before Aristotle established his categories and exclusions, relations among areas
of knowledge, between knowledge and action, and among various
forms of discourse were quite fluid. We can sketch out a much

more expansive ground for the emergence of rhetoric than Aristotle's definition allows based on the work of the first sophists in the fifth-century B.C. Though the various individual thinkers classed as "sophists" differ in the emphasis of their works, the major commentators agree that they shared goals, techniques, and outlooks and can thus be spoken of as a group (Guthrie, *Sophists* 44; Untersteiner xv). When the sophists are interpreted in reference to the mythic literary tradition, to the sixth-century natural philosophers, and to the political developments of their era, a general profile emerges of a group of intellectuals (in the active sense of the term) who rejected speculation about nature as an isolated activity but rather took their own materialist anthropology as the starting point for understanding and teaching effective discourse performance in the new democratic polis (Havelock, *Temper* 155ff.). They were skeptical about a divine source of knowledge or value and focused attention on the process of group decision-making in historically and geographically specific contexts. The first linguistic theorists, the sophists were performers as well, following in the tradition of oral poetry. But they predated the establishment of sharp distinctions between the techniques and effects of poetry and language use in other fields. Beginning, then, with an expanded and epistemologically specified "classical tradition," this history takes the whole pattern of thought of the first sophistic to define the "rhetorical" and makes it the grounds for analyzing histories of rhetoric, rhetorical theory, and composition pedagogy.

The aim of this study is to seek "rhetoric" in the comprehensive epistemic sense described above in several areas relevant to the current field of rhetoric/composition, dislodging the implicit control of "philosophic" thought inherited from Aristotle and Plato. Using the sophists as the locus of the rhetorical will allow for a focus on the general opposition of rhetoric to classical philosophy at a number of sites.[13] One of these is history. The first chapter looks not only at the fate of the sophists *in* history, but to their own historicist writing to develop a theory *of* history for rhetoric. Only within the last two centuries have historians begun to reassess the sophists from within the "philosophical" perspective. The restoration of good opinion began in the nineteenth century with Hegel, who saw the sophists as a necessary, skeptical antithesis to the Presocratics, eventually synthesized in the idealism of Plato. A few decades later in England, historian George Grote reevaluated the sophists from a utilitarian point of view in the famous chapter 67 of his multi-volume history of Greece. The argument between the British and German views was continued throughout the century in later editions of Grote and in the Hegelian history of Eduard Zeller. In our own century, at least a half dozen scholars have acknowledged the importance of the sophistic project. The most extreme in his claims for their depth and originality is Italian Mario Untersteiner (*The Sophists*, 1951). Eric A. Havelock pointed out their political significance for the democracy (*The Liberal Temper in Greek Politics*, 1957). Classicists W. K. C. Guthrie and G. B. Kerferd have provided more recent, extensive, and well-balanced treaments of the sophists (*The Sophists*, 1973; *The Sophistic Movement*, 1981). Building on these classical texts, historians in rhetoric have begun to reassess the sophists on several fronts. My own re-vision draws on the historical bent in sophistic thought as a way of reconceiving the very process of writing histories.

The narratives spun out in the longest sophistic fragments are all mythic/historical: Gorgias's *Encomium of Helen*, Protagoras's "Great Speech" about Prometheus, and Prodicus's allegory of Heracles. These forms adumbrate a central feature of the contemporary critical scene: a self-consciousness about the literary quality of any historical creation (White, "Fictions"). Indeed, the sophists can be reread for a more complex understanding about what it means to write a history, i.e., toward a historiography for rhetoric as a field today. Reinterpreting the stylistic features of antithesis and parataxis as modes of organization in the texts of Gorgias and Protagoras, I propose an approach to the writing of history more akin to a Nietzschean "genealogy" (Foucault, "Nietzsche") than to the prevailing notion of history as science—a theory-free process of collecting "facts" from the "real" world of the past. I argue that the sophists' imaginative reconstruction of their mythic past sheds light on their own current social and political problems and is a usable model for contemporary historians of rhetoric.

Having analyzed previous histories and then having proposed a historiographical method, I will try out that method on contemporary concerns in the field of composition/rhetoric in the remaining three chapters. Perhaps the most controversial reintroduction of classical issues for rhetoric and composition studies comes out of the orality/ literacy arguments of Eric A. Havelock (*Preface to Plato* and *The Literate Revolution*) and Walter Ong. The former radically revises the timing of literacy in Greece, and both draw sweeping conclusions about its implications for cognitive structures. This view of literacy is built on a commonplace of ancient history: the transformation of a "mythic" world-view through the fifth-century revolution to rationality. The work of Snell, Dodds, Solmsen, and others elaborates the changes in language and thought within the framework of an opposition between two worlds: epic and philosophic. The orality adherents describe the so-called shift from *mythos* to *logos* as a major restructuring of cognition resulting from the growth of literacy (Ong 78ff.). According to Havelock, Plato condemned *mythos,* meaning the poetic transfer of crucial cultural information, because of its hypnotic effects, arguing that it fostered an uncritical absorption of the dominant ideology (*Preface*). Instead, Plato recommended the hard mental work of dialectical thinking as an objective process. Despite the dramatic complexity of his dialogues and his own use of narrative, the heritage of Platonic thought in the Western tradition is one which reduces his rich "literary" corpus to a straightforward philosophical program from which "literature" is excluded.

This prejudice against *mythos* in a broad sense has become a central feature of the philosophic tradition, a feature by which rhetoric is tainted early on. Aristotle's major contribution to rhetoric, the systematization of informal logic, takes shape alongside the more stable structure of his formal logic. That is, the rhetorical proofs are often seen, especially from the point of view of philosophy or science, as inferior, incomplete distortions of the purer logic of the *Organon,* and the hypotactic structure of formal logic becomes the distinguishing feature of rational discourse. While Aristotle does provide for the element of *pathos* in persuasive situations, he still brackets literary performance and response off from rhetoric, and separates those from "science." Classical historians generally credit the sophists with contributing to the eventual development of a formal logic (Dodds, Solmsen, Kerferd), but the sophists' efforts remain colored by the "irrationality" of mythic structure and effect. Because their work occurs exactly on the cusp of what is described in many histories as a shift from a mythic to a logical discourse field, the relationship of their rhetoric to those fields needs specification. The second chapter will reassess the place of rhetoric within the *mythos/logos* antithesis, exploring the uses of logic in Homeric epic and the status of narrative and its attendant effects in the sophists' "rational" rhetoric. Their interest in *nomos*, custom-law, will be read as an alternative analytic to the *mythos/logos* antithesis. Emerging from the democractic spaces of local habitats, the historical process of codifying such contingent "laws" suggests a more flexible discourse and cognitive structure than those defined by the orality/literacy adherents within the literate, logical pole.

Clearly, my reading of the sophists' rhetoric in conflict with a "philosophic" tradition borrows from deconstruction the critique of binary structures. But reviving the sophists does not lead to an ahistorical exercise in proving that texts in rhetoric and composition contain internal contradictions. The feminist appropriation of deconstruction as a search for historically located and politically significant difference more adequately describes my practice (Poovey; Moi). Because Plato's exclusion of rhetoric in favor of philosophy stands as a prototype for the process of displacement that characterizes binary logic in Western philosophy, the deconstructive method that reveals and questions such displacements seems especially appropriate for a revision of the history of rhetoric. In opening up the process by which an opposition such as rhetoric/philosophy is created, deconstruction "makes visible the artifice necessary to establish, legislate, and maintain hierarchical thinking" (Poovey 13). While deconstructive practice often refuses to acknowledge its own location in history, feminist deconstructors such as Poovey find in it the potential for a "genuinely historical practice—one that could analyze and deconstruct the specific articulations and institutionalizations of . . . categories [such as rhetoric and philosophy], their interdependence, and the uneven processes by which they have been deployed and altered" (12). It is this historically sensitive deconstructive method I explore in a third chapter, positing a parallel between "women's writing" as defined by French feminist Cixous and the sophistic style as a starting point.

What is the value of rereading the sophists for teachers of writing today? As an enabling tool of the democracy, sophistic rhetoric supported a radical alternative to the monarchic and oligarchic traditions of government preceding the fifth-century Greek democracy. Historians have read the sophists as proponents of individualism and as language technicians—approaches with obvious connections to available composition pedagogies. Critiquing both these views of the sophists, I will argue in a fourth chapter that analyzing the relationships among their social theory, their pedagogy, and the functioning of the democracy in their time can lead to a more pointedly political evaluation of the teaching of writing in our own. Though the sophistic decision-making process may look like today's liberal, consensus-based politics, its critical capacity for exposing the contradictions inherent in dominant discourse suggests its relevance for literacy teachers today who seek ways to draw out minority voices. Recovering the sophists' processes of argument within their own political moment is worth pursuing toward the end of challenging hierarchies in discourse and in the institutions those hierarchies keep in place.

REREADING THE *Sophists*
CLASSICAL RHETORIC
REFIGURED

1

The past is a disputed area.

Marge Piercy, *Woman on the Edge of Time*

THE FIRST SOPHISTS:
HISTORY AND HISTORIOGRAPHY

BOTH THE written remains of the first sophists and the ancient commentary on them are minimal: only enough to fill one modest volume (Sprague; Freeman). But despite the very fragmentary nature of their surviving work and its relative neglect for centuries, the fifth-century sophists have been submitted, within the last two hundred years, to a number of historical reconsiderations. The relatively recent revival of the first sophists as a legitimate subject for historical analysis, combined with the obscurity of their work, has opened for twentieth-century scholars from a number of disciplines a wide door for interpretation and reconstruction. Discovering the significance of these histories for the emerging field of composition and rhetoric requires an examination of the ways historians of the last two centuries have redrawn the maps which are the sophists, refilling those fragmentary sketches with new detail. On a more self-reflexive level, rediscovering the sophists opens the possibility for examining the ways histories are written. My aim in this chapter will be two-fold: to examine histories *of* the sophists and history *in* the sophists.

A Dark Shadow

Until the nineteenth century, the first sophists had been buried under two millennia of neglect, an outcome of the passionate condemnation they provoked from two of their contemporaries who have fared better in the histories, Plato and Aristotle. In the several Platonic dialogues in which sophists play important roles—among them *Gorgias, Protagoras, Phaedrus*—Plato casts them as self-important, materialistic, even violent in contrast to a self-effacing, virtuous Socrates. Aristotle seconded this moral censure when he opened the *Rhetoric* as a challenge to the sophists, i.e., "framers of current treatises on rhetoric" (1354a13), who according to Aristotle are concerned only with manipulating the emotions of a judge—"warp[ing] a carpenter's rule before using it" (1354a16, 24–26). Indeed, he defines the word "sophist" explicitly in terms of "a certain kind of moral purpose" (1355b16–17), signifying by it those orators who rely completely on tricky emotional appeals rather than on a methodical investigation of the types of argument applicable to a case (1355b11–12). Thus a pattern of opposition was set. Despite the ways in which the two later Greeks appropriated features of the first sophists, the power of a simple, moral contrast between the sophists and Plato/Aristotle has infected the history of thought for centuries.[1]

The sophists' rejection of transcendent truths and eternal values, their ability to move a popular audience with a range of rhetorical techniques, their interest in social exigencies: all formed a dark "shadow" of timeless Platonic idealism and the frozen perfection of Aristotelian logic. There is much about the well-known lore of their historical existence which contributes to the impression of "otherness." They were all aliens, stranger-guests to Athens, who impressed its citizens with their expertise as diplomats, teachers, and performers. But they could be victims of fickle public opinion. Protagoras, perhaps the first self-acclaimed agnostic, may have been put out to sea in exile, his books having been burned in a public square (Sprague 5–7). The sophists were said to be intellectually meretricious, performing feats of verbal trickery and enchantment. Hippias claimed to be able to recite from memory lists of words after one look (Sprague 94–95); both he and Gorgias bragged that they could talk impromptu on any topic (Sprague 31, 97) and entranced audiences with dazzling figures and prose rhythms (Sprague 95; de Romilly 9). Their fee-taking offered another moral contrast with Plato's view of higher education as an aristocratic obligation (Marrou 33). Gorgias purportedly made enough money through his teaching to have a solid gold statue of himself made at his death (Sprague 37), and Hippias bragged that he earned more than any other pair of sophists (Plato, *Hippias Major* ¶282DE, quoted in Sprague 96). In contrast to the detached aristocrats Plato and Aristotle, the sophists in these unverifiable reports take on almost monstrous qualities of greed, exhibitionism, and deceit. The temptation to accept this exaggerated collection of impressions as a "sophistic" character has been encouraged by the generations of teachers, performers and philosophers following the first sophists who shared their label but only varying degrees of intellectual respectability (Isocrates, *Antidosis* 184 n.d; *Against the Sophists*, 162 n.b). The moral, artistic, and intellectual "otherness" of the sophists is comprehended in a profoundly influential disciplinary exclusion: Plato cast the whole field of rhetoric in the shadow of philosophy (*Phaedrus* ¶272). Jasper Neel explains how this strategy works for the benefit of Western philosophy:

> Rejecting Protagoras, Gorgias, and all their followers as relativistic nihilists whose ideas would lead to social decay, sexual perversity, and anarchy creates a comfortable certainty for Western thought. By rejecting sophistry, Western thought can play itself out as a history in which truth, after much tribulation, triumphs through its own self-righteous virtue and then remains available in the West forever. (205)

This exclusion has operated not only historically, but historiographically. That is, the domination of Platonic and Aristotelian judgments on the sophists have determined the ways the histories about them have been written.

Today the denial of the disgraceful "other" is being replayed in the academy between the poles of literary study and the teaching of composition. Belletristic authority began to replace "philosophic" at the end of the eighteenth century in the oppression of rhetoric (Howell 714 passim), a movement completed with the evolution of modern departments of English at the end of the nineteenth century.[2] The challenge to the dominance of literary criticism in departments of English posed by the emergence of composition as a distinct and legitimate field of study in the last two decades has involved a historical dimension, taking the form of a renewal of interest in classical

rhetoric. For a whole generation of teacher/scholars, then, the first
sophists become not only founders of the field but a potential locus
for psychological identification for better or worse. The kind of
revaluation of the first sophists virtually demanded by current disciplinary developments can be traced back to their "rediscovery" by
Hegel in the nineteenth century. From that moment, their potential as
the basis for a historical challenge to a dominant mode of intellectual
activity began to be exploited.

Revival and Revisions

Only a century and a half ago, in his *Lectures in the History
of Philosophy* (published posthumously in 1832), Hegel rescued the
sophists from obscurity, bringing them back within the pale of serious
historical treatment. He took the sophists' relativism as an antithesis
to the naturalism of the Presocratics in his famous dialectical view of
history. Hegel's reinterpretation seems to open a space for future
historians to reconsider the sophists more seriously than before. Since
Hegel's resurrection, these earliest inventors of rhetoric have offered
a curiously tempting slate onto which numbers of scholars have
inscribed their own programs. Indeed, throughout the nineteenth
century the site of the sophistic/Platonic crossing proved a fertile
ground for the enactment of intellectual battles.

The particular forms of thought which were inscribed onto the
poles "Plato" and "sophists" in the nineteenth century have been
outlined carefully in Frank M. Turner's *The Greek Heritage in Victorian Britain* and in the first half of volume 3 of W. K. C. Guthrie's
history of Greek philosophy, published separately as *The Sophists* (9–
13). In general terms, Plato was taken up by Hegelian idealists, such
as German historian Eduard Zeller, and British liberal Anglicans
against the British rationalist restorations of the sophists, appearing
in the histories of George Henry Lewes and George Grote (Turner,
chapter 6). Zeller, like Hegel, took the sophists' relativism as an
antithesis preceding Plato's synthesis in "high moral law." While he
felt that the group had been misrepresented in the past, he ultimately
judged them in terms of a more stringently "scientific," and thus, in

his estimate, ethical epistemology: i.e., by Platonic standards. Of course, he found them lacking. Positivist Lewes and banker Grote, however, valued the sophists' philosophical skepticism and their practical ability to effect agreement among members of social groups. Grote's massive history of Greece made the most striking impact on British intellectuals in mid-century. The phenomenon of historical "re-vision" operated on quite a literal level for classicist Henry Sidgwick, who describes his experience of reading Grote's famous chapter 67 on the sophists: "Before it was written the facts were all there, but the learned world could not draw the right inference: but after the point of view has once been suggested, . . . [the new] conclusions appear to me as clear and certain as anything can possibly be" (288). Though both sets of nineteenth-century interpreters acknowledged key elements of sophistic thought and rhetorical practice, the difference in emphasis created two different sets of sophists. It seems natural that the sophists as outsiders in their own era would become a rallying point for the positivists, who stood in roughly the same social and intellectual relation to German idealism and the conservative intellectual establishment in England as did the sophists to Plato.

The process of rewriting the sophists begun in the nineteenth century continues in the twentieth. The question now is to what extent the history of the sophists for the contemporary field of rhetoric and composition will be written through the glass of Platonic and Aristotelian modes of thought. Eric Havelock wrote *The Liberal Temper in Greek Politics* to correct just such a problem in the history of Greek political theory, thus far "written in modern times exactly as Plato and Aristotle would have wished it to be written" (18). Because Aristotle's remains the earliest and most thorough extant formulation of a rhetorical art, Havelock's description fits the early historical work in rhetorical studies, written just as Aristotle might have wished (see Introduction on Kennedy, Kinneavy, and Corbett). But a growing number of scholars have begun to narrate a different version of the history of rhetoric through a closer look at the sophists. The radically different uses of the sophists in previous eras suggest that we can discover something about our own intellectual and political climate by assessing the ways the sophists are being presented in contemporary work in composition and rhetoric. Three approaches to the sophists in the current context both reflect and project significant movements in composition studies.[3]

One approach aims at historical legitimation. Classicists Guthrie and Kerferd, followed by historians of rhetoric Richard Enos and John Poulakos, see their task primarily as establishing the sophists as serious thinkers. Of this group, the classicists identify more closely with a tradition of Anglo-American analytic philosophy, while the rhetoricians make their readers aware of the limitations of that intellectual framework. Thus, while Kerferd is able to point out that "the sophists have suffered from being set in conflict with the idealist tradition" (11), a tradition with which Guthrie is generally sympathetic, Kerferd himself tries to resist commitment to a theoretical orientation—"to avoid premature schematizations of the history of thought" (13). But this avoidance has the effect of casting his careful historical work into unexamined modes of explanation. For example, Kerferd analyzes Gorgias's treatise *On the Nonexistent* in terms of predication without questioning the history of that logical category. The persistence of Aristotelian terminology attests to the continuing necessity of re-enacting a process of legitimation. Platonic/Aristotelian modes of thought still dominate Western intellectual life to the extent that arguing for a Gorgian "epistemology" or a Protagorian "metaphysics" (Untersteiner) is still an important pre-condition for some scholars to lifting the veil of opprobrium from the sophists.

Enos confronts this problem head on in his work on Aristotle:

> Even a casual reading of this essay would reveal that this presentation has followed an Aristotelian, rational system of rhetorical composition. . . . Yet, even being a student of Aristotelian composition with years of training in rational argument does not inhibit a recognition of the process and advantages of indirect, sophistic rhetoric and that it has an epistemology—which is more than either Plato or Aristotle would have cared to admit let alone openly acknowledge. ("Aristotle" 20)

Though Enos seeks to legitimate the sophists in terms of the category "epistemology" (14–15), he moves outside of and beyond Aristotle when he describes sophistic discourse as "non-rational": a discourse structured by the conjunction of opposing *logoi* through which "meaning was indirectly revealed and experience heightened through artistic awareness" (10). Likewise, Poulakos moves from a project of raising the sophists up to the level of their Greek contemporaries ("Definition") to a reading based in Heideggerean phenomenology ("Possible"), calling into question the usefulness of an Aristotelian system of thought for a history of the sophists.

The most significant challenge to Western philosophy in recent decades, Derridean deconstruction, has spawned a second layer of sophistic histories. For his part, Derrida denies that his reading of Plato's *Phaedrus* is "spurred on by some slogan or password of a 'back-to-the-sophists' nature' " (108). Derrida calls on the sophists to personify a whole set of terms—writing, "monument," rhetoric—set against and devalued in relation to their opposites—speech, memory, philosophy. But for Derrida the sophists are the "*closest* other" of Plato (106, emphasis added), one inseparable side of a "leaf" that cannot exist without its opposite (115). Rather than simply advocating a return to the other side, Derrida shows how writing exists as a supplement to that closed system of binary dualities, the trap of logocentrism. Derrida will not let the sophists play the role of supplement, the outsider, the *pharmakon*—a role he saves for (the sophist) Socrates—because he needs them to represent the other side of the Platonic leaf.[4] While Derrida's project is a critique of the grounds of Western philosophy, his sophists remain trapped within its terms. Indeed, they are almost indistinguishable from Plato, who appropriates their arguments; Socrates's "schemes and concepts" issue from them (106).

Though Derrida insists that his critique comes from within a philosophical tradition, scholars in rhetoric are finding in deconstruction an alternative to the way that tradition (via Plato) belittles writing as merely a skill for communicating knowledge. Histories in this group recreate pre-philosophic sophists whose rhetoric precedes the binary divisions with which Derrida charges Plato: truth-seeking and communication, authorial presence and the orphaned text, philosophic speech and deceitful writing. Sharon Crowley was one of the first to explore the connections between sophistic rhetoric and deconstruction ("Gorgias"); her "A Plea for the Revival of Sophistry" revalues Plato's analogy of rhetoric with cooking and endorses it as a model for transactional writing. The most flamboyant practitioner of sophistic discourse in composition studies is Victor Vitanza, whose written and spoken performances celebrate antithesis, punning play with language, and the disjunctive and vitalizing impact of contradictory *logoi*. Jasper Neel's *Plato, Derrida, and Writing* provides the fullest articulation of deconstruction and composition, using the sophists as a way to define the "strong" discourse of a writing in process which challenges the "weak discourse" of philosophy.[5] The deconstructive re-vision of the sophists radically recharges the concept of "writing process" which has begun to sink into a well-traveled groove in the decades since its invention in the sixties. Further, its advocates shake up the sedate forums for publication, both oral and written, recreating in some ways the performances of the sophists themselves and gesturing toward more daring modes of language use within the field.

At the same time that deconstruction leads to re-formed performance, it calls into question knowledge/discourse configurations. Scholars in speech communication as well as in composition theory, rejecting a view of rhetoric dependent on non-verbal object-knowledge as a precondition for discourse about reality, have revived a rhetorical epistemology originating in the sophists. Robert Scott and Barry Brummet, in their founding articulations of "epistemic rhetoric," have provoked lively reactions from those unwilling to accept the extremity of the claim for rhetoric as a "way of knowing" (Scott 17).[6] Scott uses the Platonic opposition to the sophists as the historical orientation for a theory of rhetoric which overtly counters analytic epistemology. In its place he describes a mode of reasoning and decision-making which allows humans to act in the absence of certain, a priori truth, a process at the heart of which is rhetoric. In philosophy, Richard Rorty advances a similar program as a challenge to the "foundationalism" of Anglo-American analytic philosophy, though the sophists appear in *Philosophy and the Mirror of Nature* only as a footnote (157). James A. Berlin, in *Rhetoric and Reality,* helps to clarify the difference between speech/communication's "epistemic rhetoric" and the "meaning-making" school of composition scholars. He finds that the theories of Anne Berthoff and Knoblauch and Brannon derive from a concept of the subject (the writer) as authentic originator of insight and intuition, in the line of Plato and Kant, and thus fail to escape ultimately the philosophical grounds of the rhetoric they seek to depose.[7]

In recent years, those epistemological revisions concerned with a process of group deliberation and knowledge-formation in composition studies have been labeling themselves "social construction." Locating the source of knowledge about reality in the conversation of a social group, Kenneth Bruffee offers collaborative learning as the most epistemologically sound pedagogical strategy for composition classrooms, acknowledging in a note the connection to sophistic pedagogy. Patricia Bizzell has made a more direct connection between her early work on "outer directed" composition research and an "oratorical" as opposed to philosophical orientation in "Beyond Anti-Foundationalism" and in the headnotes to the sophists' writings in her anthology, *The Rhetorical Tradition* (with Bruce Herzberg). Radical critiques and extensions of collaborative learning (Myers, Trimbur), though they do not refer directly to the sophists, build on the pedagogical possibilities of sophistic discourse practices (see chapter 4). Social constructionist work in composition, in fact, is quite compatible with the anthropological perspective offered on the sophists by Havelock in *The Liberal Temper.* Both compositionists and classicist Havelock seek directly the political implications of a process of group decision-making.[8] Havelock resurrects the sophists as the earliest liberal politicians, finding in their materialistic explanations of the human species the foundation of democracy (*Liberal Temper* 19). As the first anthropologists, Anaximander and Xenophanes present a developmental picture of humans evolving from the animals—a view Plato challenged through his argument for the excellence inherited by a few men and women as sanction for an authoritarian educational and political system. Democritus and Protagoras build on their evolutionary forerunners the outlines of an analysis of the origins of human society characterized by its ability to solve problems through the creation and continuing readjustment of flexible social arrangements, the fifth-century Greek *polis* being only one manifestation of that ability rather than the ultimate form Plato describes. Sophist Protagoras sees the art of verbal persuasion as the mechanism allowing for the functioning of social organizations; he explains how group values evolve out of custom or habit as "pragmatic solutions to temporal and historical needs" (*Temper* 253). The only permanent reality is the historical process through which social structures and the values which undergird them are developed.

These three orientations toward the sophists signal important directions in rhetoric and composition studies at the present time. The legitimators helped to reopen the question of history-writing itself; they lead to historiographical questions. A deconstructive revision of the sophists introduces issues of speech and writing and leads into speculation about contemporary literary and rhetorical theories. The anthropological perspective brings the sophists into a political frame with radical pedagogy. Each of these engagements with the sophists has begun only within the last few years to send out ripples of change into the contemporary field of rhetoric and composition. In the chapters to follow, I will speak to those changes, beginning here with a closer look at how the sophists might change the way we view history writing itself.

Toward a Sophistic Historiography

Though the fragments of the sophists contain less direct historical reflection than the more complete texts of Plato or Aristotle, they can be identified far more than their successors with an explicitly historical mode of thought.[9] Tracing the sources of that historicism and seeking its presence in sophistic narratives will not only suggest a direction for history-writing in rhetoric today, but also make an important case for the epistemological necessity of historical modes of thinking in the new field of rhetoric/composition.[10]

The overlap of rhetoric and history in the work of the first sophists evolves from the speculations of certain Presocratic philosophers who represent what Havelock calls the "biological-historical" view of human existence and institutions, a view which takes historical contingency as the crucial defining feature of the species (*Temper* 30–31). These Greek anthropologists—Anaximander and Xenophanes in the sixth century B.C.; Anaxagoras, Archelaus, and Democritus in the fifth—understood not only physiology but also cultural mores as changing products of evolutionary process (*Temper* 104f.) Theirs is a basically diachronic understanding of human existence and stands in opposition to the ahistorical, "religious-metaphysical" orientation of the universalists like Pythagoras, Parmenides, and Plato. The difference between rhetoric and philosophy is a version of that opposition between the temporal and the eternal, the contingent and the universal.

Of special interest to the sophists was the range of group behaviors they observed in traveling through the Greek city-states (Guthrie, *Sophists* 55). They understood that any discourse seeking to effect action or shape knowledge must take into account those differences. Not only was it essential to judge the circumstances obtaining at the moment of an oration, its *kairos*, but even more essential was the orator/alien's understanding of the local *nomoi:* community-specific customs and laws. The sophists translated the natural scientists' observations about the temporality of human existence into a body of commentary on the use of discourse in the function of the social order: i.e., they concentrated on the power of language in shaping human group behavior explicitly within the limits of time and space. Sophistic rhetoric, then, as an instrument of social action in the *polis* was bound to the flux.

Given this definition of the sophists as "historicist" (Streuver 11), it is possible to describe a historiography for rhetoric loosely based on certain features of their thought and practice. I hope for this historiography to indicate not only the nature of the historical practice in this book but also to suggest a general basis on which histories of rhetoric might be constructed in the future: this is historiography in the subjunctive mode. In borrowing this notion from Streuver

(145), I shift the emphasis. Whereas Streuver is interested in the potential for critical distance inherent in the grammatical subjunctive, I exploit its predictive and prescriptive force, gesturing toward what could, would, and even should happen in the field. Here, rather than categorizing or critiquing histories of rhetoric, I will look to the works of the sophists themselves as a creative analog for a particular kind of historical practice.[11] Though the sophists did not write "histories" as we understand the genre today, in certain of their fragments and attributions historical representation plays a significant part. Thus both a general sophistic attitude toward history and specific examples of sophistic historical representation will provide the elements of a revised historiography for rhetoric.

The practice of a sophistic historiography would entail

1. a redefinition and consequent expansion of the materials and subject matters of rhetorical history, resulting in what today would be styled multi-disciplinarity—historical investigations on the margins of traditionally conceived disciplines;

2. the denial of progressive continuity: a conscious attempt to disrupt the metaphor of a complete and full chain of events with a *telos* in the revival of rhetoric in the twentieth century; and,

3. the employment of two pre-logical language *technai*, antithesis and parataxis, creating narratives distinguished by multiple or open causality, the indeterminacies of which are then resolved through the self-conscious use of probable arguments.

The resulting narratives will set aside "the history of rhetoric" in favor of "rhetorical histories"—provisional, culturally relevant "fictions of factual representation" (White, "Fictions").

Expanding the Sites of Rhetorical Activity

Traditional histories of rhetoric could be defined as those histories having taken as their subject matter chiefly documents explicitly calling themselves "rhetorics": i.e., pedagogical treatises concerned with the composition and delivery of persuasive orations (Kennedy, *Rhetoric;* Howell). This selection is based on a narrow definition of rhetoric as the teaching and performance of an opinion-based discourse for use in the social sphere as distinct from the poetic and the philosophical or scientific.[12] The thought and practice of the sophists themselves, however, was never so narrowly defined. They were interested in a whole group of intellectual materials and social actions, the common feature of which was language use. It might be argued that Plato and Aristotle as well exhibited such a range of interests, but the difference is that, for the sophists, all other subjects were subsumed under the rhetorical. In their works, rhetoric permeated every topic: natural science and "epistemology" (*Protagoras* B1–2; Gorgias, *On the Nonexistent* B1–5; *Prodicus* B3–4; *Antiphon* B66c), social and political theory (*Protagoras* C1; *Thrasymachus* B6a; *Antiphon* B129–151), aesthetic response and psychology (*Protagoras* B1; Gorgias, *Encomium of Helen* B11; *Antiphon* B123), law (*Protagoras* B6; *Gorgias* B11a; *Antiphon* B1–66), religion and ethics (*Protagoras* A23, B4; *Gorgias* A28), as well as language theory and pedagogy (*Protagoras* A 5, 21, 26; *Gorgias* B14).[13] Sophistic "rhetoric" collided and interbred with literature, science, and philosophy before such interests were bracketed by Aristotle as disciplines. Just as the sophists engaged in a wide range of intellectual and social activities before the constraints of Platonic/Aristotelian metaphysics and epistemology cordoned off investigations of human mental and physical behavior, so can they serve today as a point of reference for the formation of a comprehensive historical practice unfettered by strict disciplinary boundaries, a practice of history neither exclusively "intellectual" nor "social" (Schilb, "History") nor even strictly "factual" in differentiation from the fictional (White, "Fictions"). The revisionary historian today will work with an expanded range of materials: not only the pedagogical treatises summarized in traditional histories, but any literary artifact as it operates to shape knowledge and effect social action. The identification of materials at an active site becomes as much the work of the revisionary historian as her commentary on them.[14] This issue has been particularly crucial in feminist revisions of history (see Peaden). Progress toward the reformation of the field along feminist lines can be seen in the inclusion of several women in the Bizzell and Herzberg anthology, as well as a serious consideration of gender issues in their headnotes (see *The Rhetorical Tradition*).

In departments of English, the hegemony of literary studies has shaped the recent practice of history of rhetoric in several ways. The notion of history of rhetoric as a history of writing instruction has evolved naturally out of the recent revolution in writing pedagogy. Such an approach serves a genuine desire to know something about forgotten teachers and their ways while at the same time satisfying conventional disciplinary requirements for transforming "composition" into a distinct and legitimate area of study—one that can be shown to have a history. But "the history of writing instruction" as a historical backdrop for contemporary composition/rhetoric is a definition with drawbacks, as well, for both composition and literature. Literary scholars, under such an arrangement, can keep the new co-habitant of the "English" department from usurping already well-staked turf (Harkin, "Reifying"). At the same time this narrow definition of rhetoric also keeps in place an equally narrow view of "literature" (Eagleton).

The movement from a disciplinary "history of rhetoric" to a post-disciplinary rhetorical historiography demands an expansion of the field of study. A disruption of categories like "literature," while potentially politically troublesome, must become an essential feature of a revised rhetorical historiography. "Rhetoric" at its most fruitful has historically functioned as a meta-discipline through which a whole spectrum of language uses and their outcomes as social action can be refracted for analysis and combination (see Phelps, "Domain"). In terms of physical evidence and pedagogical practice, the point is most radically to reconsider the notion of a canon. The rhetorician has from the beginning been a generalist. The goal for the historian in an age of vast and highly specialized knowledge should become neither the mastery of a limited body of texts nor the impossible task of knowing everything and ordering it, but rather an agility in moving between disciplines, standing back from them with the critical perspective characteristic of both history and rhetoric (Streuver 197f.) for the purpose of illuminating meaningful connections, disjunctions, overlaps, or exclusions. The choice of texts for any particular history will become an expression of *ethos;* the historian makes a case for the relevance of a particular combination of materials based on her practical understanding of the issues involved, an ethical commitment, and good judgment about the best interests of the audience. Already rhetorical historians are beginning to venture outside the most limited version of what constitutes "rhetoric" and into other areas. Berlin (*Writing*) and Covino have taken on traditionally literary figures Emerson and DeQuincey; LeFevre includes Freud and Kant in a study of invention; Campbell and Bazerman engage in rhetorical investigations of scientific discourse with studies of Darwin and contemporary physicists. Striking examples of the direction rhetorical histories could take are pointed by Foucault's studies of madness (*Madness*), sexuality (*History*), and prisons (*Discipline*); G. E. R. Lloyd's investigations of linguistic structures, science, and folklore in ancient Greece (*Magic*); and the work of Michel Serres.

While the general historicism of the first sophists suggests an attitude toward history, two texts from the period provide a model for the practice of rhetorical historiography. In both Gorgias's *Encomium of Helen* and the "Great Speech" of "Protagoras" in Plato's dialogue,[15] a multiplicity of subjects comprehended under rhetoric are interwoven into a historical narrative. *Helen,* an argument seeking to deny her responsibility in starting the Trojan War, offers speculation on morals, the psychology of reception, the relation between sense impressions and language; Protagoras's retelling of the Prometheus myth in response to Socrates's question about teaching virtue takes into consideration the origin and development of the species, language, pedagogy, and social philosophy. It could be argued that such discourses are irrelevant to the modern situation because of the differences in genre. The encomium and the parable, though both contain elements common to history, have histories of their own as genres. I would respond that a recuperation of literary sub-genres congruent to history as a strict empirical science would not be a fruitless enterprise for rhetorical historians, for whom an expansion of materials may suggest a concomitant reconsideration of generic categories.[16]

Perhaps an even more troublesome problem for the contemporary historian in accepting these two discourses as models for history
writing is their mythic status: the raw material for both histories is
what we would today take to be exclusively "literary" or "fictional."
But in both discourses what is more significant than establishing
irrefutable facts is the choice of a historical incident for its usefulness
in the reconstruction and interpretation of culturally meaningful and
instructive pasts. The opportunities for speculation provided by the
narrative situation in each case—on the power of *logos* in *Helen* and
on the role of language in our evolution as a species in *Protagoras*—
supersedes the establishment of the "factual" status of the materials
themselves as a goal for the discourse. I certainly would not suggest
that rhetorical historians fabricate a past that never existed but rather
note that a view of history as merely uncovering lost "facts" doesn't
take fully enough into account the inevitably literary or mythic quality
of any historical reconstruction and its relevance to the present. The
use of these sophistic historical arguments as analogs for a contemporary historical practice is intended to encourage an increased self-
consciousness about that process of reconstruction as it functions to
open for investigation fruitful questions about belief, purpose and
self-definition rather than answer questions of "fact."[17]

The Disruption of Progressive Continuity

In each sophistic discourse, the retelling of a well-known story
throws into question existing versions. Gorgias casts doubt on Hel-
en's responsibility for the Trojan War; Protagoras's Prometheus
stands in sharp contrast to earlier characterizations. Whereas both
Hesiod's and Aeschylus's narratives about Prometheus culminate in
the conflict between the Titan and Zeus, the sophist downplays that
outcome and focuses on the god's concern for the fate of the human
species. Each sophistic discourse disrupts a stable historical narrative
and subverts the teleology of its analogs. Gorgias's retelling of the
abduction of Helen explicitly throws into question the moral censure
of her behavior:

> Helen [is] a woman about whom the testimony of inspired po-
> ets has become univocal and unanimous as had the ill omen of her
> name, which has become a reminder of misfortunes. For my part . . .
> I wish to free the accused of blame and, having reproved her de-
> tractors as prevaricators and proved the truth, to free her from their
> ignorance. (Sprague 50)

In so doing, the sophistic historian disrupts the continuity of the given historical narrative which uses Helen to take the blame for what could be re-seen as a disastrous adventure driven by the violent logic and *ethos* of a phallocentric culture. By pulling out that crucial link in the sequence of events leading to the war, Gorgias opened up the causal chain, not only implicitly calling into question the historical reasons for her condemnation but, more important, introducing new issues of significance in the present as a consequence: questions about the relations or similarities between love and force, language and love, language and force. Consciously refusing to tell history as a continuous, complete narrative leading to a pre-understood end, the sophist was able to throw into new light a range of facts and causes for the purpose of a more general consideration. Others have de- scribed the sophists' historicism in complementary ways. Streuver associates sophistic rhetoric with a historical practice which continu- ally redefines rather than affirms pre-existing definitions. Havelock links the sophists with a school of historical writers including first- century A.D. Diodorus Siculus who attempted projects which did not lend themselves to strong thematic structure (*Temper* 73).

NOTE

The issues of continuity and teleology are complicated in the case of Protagoras's Promethean myth by the fact that it is ultimately Plato's discourse. Havelock's sensitive reading of the story in three stages offers a convincing method for extracting what can be verified as the sophistic elements in the narrative through comparison with other sources. In the first stage of "Protagoras's" story, the brothers Prometheus and Epimetheus are assigned the task of distributing faculties to the various creatures at the time of creation. Epimetheus thoughtlessly gives away all the qualities of physical strength and protection, so his foresightful brother steals fire and, more important, the technological skill humans needed to use it . The second stage of the story finds humans building cities, using language, tilling the soil, but still in danger of extinction by wild beasts and war among themselves. At this moment, Zeus intervenes in the evolutionary development, bestowing divine gifts of justice and respect and instructing Hermes to distribute them equally among humans, though technical skill had not been so distributed. Havelock argues that the third stage can be read as Plato's co-opting of what began as an anthropological account of human development for a defense of inborn excellence as the basis of an aristocratic political order (*Temper* 87–94). Though there is no way of knowing how the historical Protagoras would have carried on the story, his well-known agnosticism makes it is reasonably certain that his account would not have included the intercession of a divine force. Though Havelock sees in Protagoras's portion of the story an evolutionary continuity leading to a justification for a democratic political structure, that very use of the Prometheus myth, I would argue, represents a "revision" of the other versions—Hesiod's, Aeschylus's, and Plato's—in each of which human creation and development is delimited by and culminates in the authority of Zeus.[18]

The point for a modern rhetorical historiography is the disruption of the conventional expectation that a history be a complete, replete, full, and logically consistent narrative record. The ancient idea of the Great Chain of Being, much older even than its eighteenth-century revival, is still a contending epistemological metaphor in the twentieth century. While the positivism of the nineteenth century removed the necessity for a transcendent source for order, the desire for "data" which fill in a pre-formulated hypothesis remains strong. Not only is the chain full, but it has direction. For historical practice, the model dictates the location of every datum on a ladder advancing up to or down from a certain culminating point (see North 78).

For rhetorical historians, the point of breaking the chain, of resisting the impulse to fit historical materials into a neat, continuous line from beginning to end, is to achieve the kind of critical distance which allows for re-vision. Rather than attempting to trace a line of thought from A to B, the rhetorical historian will seek to regroup and redefine. The point is to expose an increasing *complexity* of evidence or data, to resist the simplification which covers over subtleties, to exploit complexity toward the goal of greater explanatory power. The revisionary historian of rhetoric will not look for superficial similarities which group themselves quickly into "species" but will persist in confounding categories by looking longer and discovering finer and finer shades of difference—more and more varieties. She will see the sophist in Plato, Augustine, and Bacon; the hidden Platonist in Nietzsche.

There are several candidates for metaphors to replace the chain or ladder. Foucault argues in "The Discourse on Language" for the replacement of continuities with "events and series" combined through a theory of "discontinuous systematization" (230–31). He represents this process figuratively as cutting a "slice" or finding a "staging post" (232)—metaphors similar to White's figuration of "contextualist" historical arguments as those which "incline more toward synchronic representations of segments or sections of the process, cuts made across the grain of time as it were" (*Metahistory* 19). The problem is describing a historical practice which denies both "mechanically causal links and an ideal necessity" among events (Foucault, "Discourse" 231). Nietzsche offers the notion of "genealogy" in contrast to history as a solution—a concept which receives its most powerful articulation in Darwin's evolutionary theory. Though Foucault, in reading Nietzsche on history, discredits "evolution" as an attempt to "map the destiny of a people" ("Nietzsche" 146), Darwin's reading of natural history exactly parallels Foucault's description of a proper historical practice: "To follow the complex course of descent is to maintain passing events in their proper dispersion; it is to identify the accidents, the minute deviations—or conversely, the complete reversals—the errors, the false appraisals, and the faulty calculations that gave birth to those things that continue to exist and have value for us" ("Nietzsche" 146).[19] Stephen Jay Gould's pedestrian metaphor for Darwinian historiography—the bush—offers a strong contender to replace the ladder as a way of re-seeing events both within their complex relations diachronically and in series through time. Any one of the multitude of possible revisionary reconstructions will follow a "circuitous path running like a labyrinth, branch to branch, from the base of the bush to a lineage now surviving at its top" (Gould 61).

The differences in outcome between a traditional or continuous history and a discontinuous alternative can be observed by contrasting a strictly philosophic view of the sophists with the more revisionary alternatives outlined earlier in the chapter. On the "ladder" view, the first sophists' stylistic innovations provided the raw materials for Plato's dialectic and later Aristotle's logic of non-contradiction. Their emotional appeals and arguments from probability were systematized and legitimated by Aristotle's *Art*. In short, they are significant as a link between the oral society of the archaic period and the literate flowering in the fourth century B.C. These explanations are recognizable as commonplaces of traditional histories of rhetoric. But reconsidered as a branch of a bush, they become the practitioners of a rhetoric which represents an independent and legitimate alternative response to the particular environment of the fifth-century B.C. Greek city-states—materialist, anthropological, "historical," "liberal," pragmatic. They become a source for analysis of a number of subsequent historical moments, such as Renaissance humanism (Streuver) and the "post-literate" media age of late-twentieth-century America (Corcoran).

What has led to such revisions and what emerges as a feature of a number of contemporary historiographical theories is the necessity for overturning givens: those sequences of events which have through repetition evolved from "truth" into truism. This impulse toward iconoclasm is variously described by Nietzsche as "critical history" ("Uses" 67), by Foucault as reversal ("Discourse" 229), by White as the ironic mode (*Metahistory* 433). In such histories, Foucault warns, "one can already be pretty sure that the stresses will not fall where we expect, and that taboos are not always to be found where we imagine them to be" ("Discourse" 232). The sophists' employed a verbal *techne* instrumental in effecting that critical, revisionary turn: antithesis. The stylistic device of setting in sequence opposing grammatical and lexical structures can operate at a deeper level of narrative

construction and causal linkage as an instrument of rhetorical historical practice.

Antithesis and Parataxis: History in the Tragi/Comic Mode

The first two features of revisionary history—the broad range of
materials and the denial of progressive continuity—complicate issues
of "logical" structure and causal connection in historical narrative.
Method becomes crucial and problematic under a reconsidered project of history. Here the legacy of the sophists is quite specific at the
level of syntax. Their discursive practice suggests a two-stage process
of historical composition—a tragic dissolution consonant with the
iconoclastic movement of critical or ironic historiography followed
by a "comic" reconstruction. Of the two syntactic structures therein
employed, antithesis creates an openness to the multiplicity of possible causal relations, then parataxis demands the employment of probable arguments in the reconstitution of provisional historical narratives.

Under a traditional historiography, the sophists' uses of antithesis—playfully pairing opposite words—are interpreted in two ways.
First, they are seen as a manipulative device for eliciting emotional
effects in oratorical performance: the antithetical style creates "a tin-
tinnabulation of rhyming words and echoing rhythms" with hypnotic
effect on listening crowds (Kennedy, *Rhetoric* 29). Second, in the
development of logic, antithesis becomes a precursor to Socratic
definition and, eventually, to an Aristotelian logic of noncontradic-
tion, both of which work because they *exclude* one of the two options
(Kerferd; Guthrie, *Sophists*). Even in Solmsen's lengthy, serious treatment of the sophists' "intellectual experiments" (83–125), the assumption of a split between form and content leads to a generally suspicious
attitude toward antithesis defined as a pre-logical stylistic device. For
example, he describes Thucydides's use of the *techne* as an "idiosyn-
crasy" (110), an "addiction" (84), something he is "not above" (84).

But other historians have introduced possibilities for interpreting
antithesis extending beyond those traditional explanations. John Fin-

ley's analysis of Thucydides's style acknowledges a more significant conceptual role for the *techne*. In arguing for a chronology of influence, Finley traces an increasing sophistication in its use from Homer to the earliest prose writers through Sophocles and Euripides and finally to the sophists. Though Finley discredits Gorgias as pressing antithesis to its "illogical conclusion" (112), he sees its use by others as fostering an expanding capacity for more complex generalization (109). Untersteiner goes further, describing the introduction of paired opposites as a Gorgian "tragic" sense of knowledge (101–161). Under this revisionist view, antithesis is not a spurious trick for clouding the minds of the listeners but rather works to awaken in them an awareness of the multiplicity of possible truths.[20] The sophistic historian will not "confine reality within a dogmatic scheme but allow it to rage in all its contradictions, in all its tragic intensity" (Untersteiner xvi). The sophists, fully capable of understanding a logic of non-contradiction, were less concerned with the "scientific" project of establishing a formal logic than with exploring social consequences of logical moves (e.g., in the problems with communication in Gorgias's *On the Nonexistent*) and possibilities for interpreting past events in light of present needs (Poulakos, "Possible").

Both the *Encomium of Helen* and the *Defense of Palamedes* are arguments without conclusions: they organize probabilities toward the end of reinterpreting elements of mythic history. In these attempts, Gorgias employs antithesis not as a dissolvent force in language but rather to establish the conditions for constructing socially functional, but always provisional, rhetorical speculations. Gorgias's revision of the story of Helen of Troy exemplifies the function of antithesis in the establishment of complex causal relations. In the speech he puts into play a quartet of possible causes for the abduction, any two of which could be set up as an antithesis: fate/love, love/force, force/persuasion, persuasion/love, etc. But rather than excluding three causes in favor of one, setting up a necessary chain of causal relation, Gorgias focuses the discussion on the interplay among causes, the interrelation of the four.[21] In this case, Gorgias insists upon an indeterminacy, or even an overdeterminacy, of situation in order to speculate on the power of *logos*—a force coming to be seen in the mid-fifth century Greek *polis* as rivaling the fate of the gods or even physical violence in its power. Because of the gap between the reality of deeds—past, present, and future—and the words which represent them, any persuasion has an element of deception (Rosenmeyer, de Romilly, *Magic*). Thus Helen "against her will, might have come under the influence of speech, just as if ravished by the force of the mighty" (Sprague 52). Though *logos* lacks the power of fate, it takes the same form, "constraining the soul . . . both to believe the things said and to approve the things done." The parallel between verbal persuasion and the desire created by a pleasing visual impression works as a third means of exploring the psychology of *logos* (Segal). At one point, Gorgias playfully suggests the scheme of a sophistic historiography, implicitly challenging the conventions of factual, continuous history, historical time, and simple cause/effect relations:

> Who it was and why and how he sailed away, taking Helen as his love, I shall not say. To tell the knowing what they know shows it is right but brings no delight. Having now gone beyond the time once set for my speech, I shall go on to the beginning of my future speech, and I shall set forth the causes through which it was likely that Helen's voyage to Troy should take place. (Sprague 51)

The importance of pleasure in the telling and the reference to the future indicate purposes for Gorgias's history, as well as creating a link between probabilities for past actions and prospects for future ones. At the end of the speech, none of the four is identified as the single, or even primary cause. Antitheses have evolved into complex interrelations.

Thus Gorgias's "encomium" is capable of interpretation in terms of a historiographical method. Laying out a number of causes for a past event is taken as the occasion for exploring issues of vital importance for the present and future. In Gorgias's hands history becomes not the search for the true, but an opening up of questions: an enterprise not so much of reaching conclusions but of uncovering possible contradictions. Antithesis as more than a mere stylistic gesture disrupts previous complacent givens without, in this case, offering a clear resolution. One might read that lack of resolution as a necessary feature of Gorgias's project as a democratic diplomat and politician during the last third of the fifth century, which saw the beginning of the Second Peloponnesian War in 431 and the death of Pericles in 429. In that unstable time the rhetor, like his contemporary, the historian Thucydides, may have sought to call into question simpler causal explanations of the past in favor of opening up alternative possibilities to account for the confusing turbulence of the present (Thucydides 35, 49).[22]

While the example of Gorgias as rhetorical historian corresponds to the descriptions of critical history cited earlier, the lack of resolution fails to signal a directive for action. Removing the blame from Helen entails a reconsideration of values, but the rhetorical historian both then and now has a strong obligation to action in the social and pedagogical world. A second syntactic structure characteristic of sophistic discourse balances the analytic effect of antithesis with a synthetic gesture which, nonetheless, remains flexible—free from the tighter bonds of a "logical" alternative. Parataxis, the loose association of clauses without hierarchical connectives or embedding, is, under traditional explanations, a language behavior typical of primitive story-telling: a less sophisticated organization than its opposite, hypotaxis, the highest expression of which is Aristotelian propositional logic. But again extended beyond the level of mere style, parataxis can suggest a kind of historical practice complementary to the dissolvent impulse of antithesis alone.

The discourse of the character "Protagoras" illustrates the role of parataxis in historical argument: through the narrative *techne* he moves beyond the critical to the constructive (Untersteiner 57–62). While antithesis functioned to overthrow a commonplace about a historical character within the encomium, parataxis arises from a different *ethos*. Though "Protagoras's" Promethean creation story actually provides a critical revision of Hesiod's cosmogony, the sophist appears to be constructing a new tale for the benefit of the young men he is invited to instruct. Not only does the choice of a paratactic style of arrangement give the story a more constructive force, it fits the progressive evolutionary historicism underpinning sophistic thought.

In the first stage, the references to materials of creation—mud and water—identify Protagoras as a successor of the anthropologists Anaximander, Xenophanes, and Democritus—all of whom advanced evolutionary theories of human origins from inanimate matter and other animals. After Epimetheus gives away all the physical features for protection, however, Prometheus steps in to "arm" humans with fire and technology. At this point, Havelock helps us to see the Platonic classificatory impulse intruding into the narrative of the sophist by interrupting the evolutionary development from animal to human, dividing with finality *aloga* (witless) creatures from *loga* humans (*Temper* 87–94). By disrupting the associative connections of parataxis, Plato removes the process from "Protagoras's" story (Havelock *Temper* 91). Not only are humans divided from animals and from the gods, but the intellectual power symbolized by fire and *techne* is separated from moral sense, supplied from above by Zeus. Plato insists on in-born excellence as the basis of political order and clear distinctions among creatures. A conclusion more consistent with Protagoras's general outlook would have discovered civic responsibility emerging through an evolutionary continuity and leading to a democratic political structure. While Protagoras would grant that everyone partakes of "civic excellence" in some degree, in his view

> the human being never begins as a political animal; he only becomes such in the course of his social evolution from the savage to the civilized condition. And his excellence correspondingly has never been a fixed and permanent quantity, but an evolving pattern of habit and response and value. (Havelock, *Temper* 170)

"Protagoras" is prevented by Plato from representing genuinely that kind of evolutionary progression in the myth. But, paradoxically, the argument "Protagoras" offers following the story establishes the conditions under which such development takes place. In it, "Protagoras" explains how the social order functions to shape its members as cooperative participants. According to Havelock, Protagoras elaborates a sophistic "theory and practice of communication" (216), which includes an "epistemology of public opinion" along with a "theory of popular cognition and decision" (220). This elaboration of a democratic mode of communication as a happy moment in the evolution of humans challenges the conservative belief in in-born excellence at the foundation of both the older warrior-culture and of Plato's utopian aristocracy; thus, the effect of "Protagoras's" discourse is both critical and constructive. As the spokesperson for democratic decision-making, Plato's "Protagoras" recommends specific pedagogical practices as natural extensions of his historical narrative: a literary study following on socialization by the family, which inculcates civic virtues (¶325–27).

That process of reformulation is itself rhetorical. In the dialogue, "Protagoras" argues that he can teach good judgment to his students because people have the capacity to decide among all the multitudinous and contradictory *logoi* available which are "better" (*kreitton*) and which "worse" (*hetton*). They develop the capacity to make such decisions through their membership in a group. Qualities of justice and respect for others have to be taught and nourished through structures of family and school. Those who do the best job of developing their social capacities are able both to recognize and to convince others of the better knowledge.

Despite the imposition of Platonic categories onto the paratactic narrative, the "Great Speech" still stands as an example of socially motivated historical reconstruction. Taking together Protagoras's fragments and his evolutionary parable, we see the sophist moving from a recognition of the contradictory nature of reality to a way of selecting from among those *logoi* certain propositions and converting them into socially useful rhetorical constructs: a "knowledge" existing within and communicated through persuasion (Untersteiner 53–55). Protagoras's theory and practice of a political rhetoric was valued highly in Periclean Athens. While Gorgias's "history" successfully opened a number of speculations through antithesis, "Protagoras" clearly recommends a course of action: a political education of each citizen of the *polis*.

The repeated movement from the tragic critique provided by antithesis to the comic reformulation of parataxis was essential for the sophists. Though they are at worst characterized as skeptics and idle bickerers, in fact they and their students did political and legal work in the *polis*. In most disciplines the space between theory and practice allows for a wider separation between critical and constructive purposes. But rhetoric, because of its commitment to action, must be able to move from critique to reconstruction. The historical discourses of Gorgias and Protagoras, as well as their lives as teachers and diplomats, illustrate that movement.[23]

Arrangement in Tragi/Comic Rhetorical History

The displacement of the "logical" structure of traditional history in favor of "narrative" structure of rhetorical history changes dramatically the status of arrangement.[24] A reconsideration of arrangement is best approached through analogy. Imagine parataxis as linear in its structure and aural in effect; hypotaxis, as vertical and visual. This analogy overturns the typical representation of inferential logic as "linear" based on the sentence as an equation. The alternative way to figure the difference takes as crucial the fact that in a propositional equation, the end is prefigured from the beginning—the whole structure is built in a vertical form, "hypo" suggesting an organization "from under."[25] The hypotactic discourse seems to exist as a complete, two-dimensional visual construct—as Platonic *eide* (appearance) or Aristotelian *theoria* (vision)—before its verbal performance; whereas discourse structured paratactically creates the effect of evolving in time, through sound striking the ears, minds, bodies of its listeners in a temporal experience. The claim is not that orally performed hypotactic discourse would not affect an auditor over the time of the speech, but rather it pretends not to—it obscures or ignores its own existence on the temporal plane while discrediting any "logical" content of the paratactic alternative.

Antithesis allows for laying out options; parataxis provides for their loose coordination in a narrative with a social rather than epistemological purpose, strictly defined. The difference between sophistic historiography and a deconstructive practice is that parataxis follows or is interwoven with antithetical dissolution. The tragic opening up is resutured in a consciously constructed story: a temporary comic resolution.[26] This concept of arrangement is not Plato's organic form, growing from inside; it is rather a human invention. The story-teller plays with the material like Frankenstein with body parts. With both antithesis and parataxis, the point is not exposing or discovering the unknown, but rearranging the known. Invention is collapsed with arrangement as a single rhetorical canon. Traditional histories of rhetoric, bound by convention, derive their force and appeal from their logical presentation. Sophistic histories, on the other hand, could introduce into twentieth-century scholarship an alternative "method" of discourse in the most literal sense of finding a new path—specifically in asserting the validity of narrative as a vehicle for the serious tasks of knowledge creation, storage, and use on a more self-conscious level than the modes of emplotment White finds in the "restricted" historical art of the nineteenth century (*Metahistory* 9).[27] A sophistic method works by exposing and exploring a range of possibilities for knowledge and action and implicitly theorizing the process of their acceptance by the community less on the basis of logical validity and more on the force of their "rhetorical," i.e., persuasive and aesthetic, appeal.[28] Rearrangement is revaluation. In sophistic history the pretense to distanced objectivity is overshadowed by an open acknowledgement of a value orientation: any realignment is made for a purpose.[29]

Rhetorical histories move along a continuum toward literary performance and away from objective collection of empirical data, which have themselves currently become subjects of analysis as discursive performances (Bazerman). Such histories are frankly imaginative reconstructions, instruments of *psychogogia* granted assent through their reception by the whole person who reads or hears them—not just on "cognitive" or "rational" grounds—and adopted because they serve social needs for the cultures out of which they arise. They self-consciously and without false modesty argue their theses, holding them up for applause and revision.

Conclusions

One primary objection to be anticipated to the historical practice outlined here comes out of the metaphysical/philosophical tradition: that such histories would neglect objective evidence and lack logical validity—the objection launched against the sophists by Plato. The goal for a rhetorical historiography would be not completely to renounce the "logical" or "factual," but to stop relying on their supremacy over their supposed opposites, to investigate a range of alternatives between those illusory poles. This historiographical goal fits with a view of writing instruction that seeks to complicate categories of fact and fiction and with feminists' challenges to a strict separation between personal experience and abstract reason (e.g., de Lauretis, "Semiotics"). Indeed, the revisionary histories of sophists reviewed above and of feminists like Mary Daly and Hélène Cixous move in the direction suggested by the historical work of the sophists themselves: a playful critique of philosophy animated by a progressive political vision.

The next chapter, in fact, explores the polarities complicated both by sophistic texts and by some histories of them. In an attempt to put into practice the method I have laid out above, I will try to unravel a portion of the master-narrative for the development of human consciousness, locating the sophists at a moment called the birth of "rationality."

2

Deeply troubled, he spoke to his own great-hearted
spirit . . .

Homer, *Iliad* XVII. 90

BETWEEN *MYTHOS* AND *LOGOS*

R EREADING the sophists demands a critical reexamination of a dominant historical trope for Western antiquity: the rational revolution of the Greek enlightenment accompanying the birth of democracy. Historians often see this movement as the end of a long progress from one form of consciousness to another—from *mythos* to *logos* (Dodds; Snell; Havelock, *Preface*). The most recent version of this trope, one with serious implications for contemporary studies in rhetoric and composition, finds expression as the orality/literacy formulation (Havelock, *Revolution* and *Preface;* Ong; Goody). These two historical models share the assumption that certain mental operations, specifically an elaborated syllogistic logic and the introspection or critical distance presumed necessary for such logic, are not possible within an "oral" or "mythic" consciousness.[1] In some versions of the theory, the democratic reforms of the late sixth and early fifth centuries play an essential role in the transformation of consciousness.

That the advent of writing initiates significant changes in the way humans think and act cannot be denied. But certain assumptions about the independent status and function of narrative and rational argument at separate moments in history can be fruitfully complicated by the introduction of rhetoric into the historical picture. Curiously absent from many discussions of the emergence of literacy and rationality in the classical period, rhetoric—and particularly sophistic rhetoric—will provide two ways of challenging the dualism of *mythos/ logos.*[2] At one end of the historical continuum, we find argument and introspection in the epic; at the other, we examine the role of myth in sophistic contributions to the rational revolution. Relocating the sophists and rhetoric in the "progress" from orality to literacy will work against the historical view of rhetoric bursting out abruptly as a rough-and-ready practice in the fifth century, to be fully realized as a theory only by the next generation. Instead, changes in the fifth century will be seen as evolutionary rather than revolutionary (Swearingen, "Literate" 154)—as an intricate interweaving of threads from earlier centuries eventually picked up by the sophists. I will first describe and then challenge the idea of a "mythic" consciousness by looking at examples of argument and mental activity in Homer. Next will come a reexamination of the role of democracy in the evolution of rhetoric over several centuries. Finally, after a brief look at some Presocratic influences, there will follow an analysis of the "mixed" discourse of two central figures in the sophistic movement, Protagoras and Gorgias. A sophistic rereading of these classical materials may disrupt the smooth, unidirectional historical flow from *mythos* to *logos*, complicating discrete categories of rational and "literary" discourse.

Language and Thought in the "Mythic" World

What is meant by a "mythic" world? The expression signifies a whole complex of features characteristic of Greek culture from Homeric times to the fifth century, many of which are pertinent to an understanding of rhetoric. While rhetoric as a formal art did not exist until the early fifth century, persuasive speaking appears in the earliest records of Greek discourse: in the Homeric epic. It will be instructive to examine what kind of rhetoric is practiced under a "mythic" framework.[3] Some selected classical scholarship (from which references to rhetoric are almost universally absent) can help fill in, or lead us to question, assumptions about the period on which we build histories of rhetoric. The most obvious defining feature of a mythic era is the myths themselves, a set of stories providing explanations of natural phenomena, detailed codes of everyday behavior, and even geographical and technological information. These myths were communicated through public recitations of the Homeric epic poems in a wide range of contexts: during religious events and competitions, in after-dinner entertainments for all classes, by teachers and students in educational settings, even around the fires of military encampments (Havelock, *Revolution* 18–19). These oral performances and the quality of consciousness they created in their audiences have become the focus of intense scrutiny by Eric A. Havelock and Walter Ong under the designation of "orality." Their work, based on the linguistic analyses of formulae in oral poetry by Milman Parry and Albert B. Lord, offers a persuasive argument for the existence of a "preliterate" mind whose operations are structured completely by the poetic form in which it received crucial information about the culture. Though it will remain to be seen to what extent the full expression of this theory can be accepted, a summary of its main features will provide a starting point for investigating language use in the centuries before the formal art of rhetoric appeared.

According to the orality scholars, audiences in "oral" cultures totally identified with the tale, lulled into a semi-hypnotic state by the regular meter of the verse (Havelock, *Preface* 159). The reciter himself was hardly more conscious, it seems; patching together well-known segments from a "generalised memory," he followed a track rather than directed it (*Revolution* 178–79). There was no question of "creating" these tales, according to the orality/literacy exponents; the thought belonged to the tradition, not the singer. The narrative of oral poetry is structured on an echo pattern, relying for unity on the thematic resemblance of episodes (*Revolution* 140–41). Links between parts of the story are paratactic, i.e., loosely associative based on temporal sequence without strong emphasis on causal relations between events. Thus the cultural instructions—*nomoi* and *ethe*—communicated through these public events came to the audience in the form of a plurality of instances, not a generalized system (*Preface* 185). Both the mode of performance and the structure of the discourse encouraged total, uncritical acceptance of the cultural code, Havelock asserts. New material was worked into the "cultural encyclopedia" only in "the shape of the typical," the present seamlessly interwoven with the past (*Preface* 123).

Havelock claims this oral cultural condition remained in place very late, until mid-fifth century B.C., and only gradually metamorphosed into its logical or literate successor. Some general dimensions of this mythic language world provide a more positive view of certain features of sophistic rhetoric judged as ethically questionable or manipulative after Plato and Aristotle. The degree of sensual pleasure associated with socially functional language acts certainly violates the Aristotelian separation between poetic and prosaic discourses. If this experience of public performance was commonplace in the eighth, seventh, and sixth centuries, the tendency for fifth-century rhetoricians to seek pleasurable effects in their new prose derives from a well-established tradition rather than representing an innovation in manipulation (Murphy, *Synoptic* 12). It is important to keep in mind the fusion of roles for the poet/minstrel in the "mythic" world: as transmitter of cultural knowledge in all areas of life, he acted like a political leader, teacher, and religious seer (Havelock, *Preface* 121).[4] Conversely, a political or spiritual leader derived his effectiveness in large part from his skill at speaking artfully. This combination of roles is borne in pre-Platonic uses of the word "sophist": a non-pejorative collection of meanings ranging from skilled craftsman to artist, statesman to teacher, poet to sage (Guthrie, *Sophists* 27–34). Though Plato would vigorously work to divide those functions—as today the poet seems far distant from both the philosopher and the politician—it is important for us to keep in mind that "in Greek eyes practical instruction and moral advice constituted the main function of the poet" (Guthrie, *Sophists* 29).[5] I labor this point because of the degree to which poetry and story-telling are today seen as tainted by a kind of irrationality, making them unsuitable means for expressing serious thought and negotiating public decisions. An impression of the sophists' place in the shift from a "mythic" to a "logical" culture requires now a closer look at the status of narrative.

For the culture of *mythos,* narrative was the structure in which world-knowledge was carried (Havelock, *Preface* 121). One compelling way to interpret this narrative knowledge comes from Havelock's reading of Plato, who condemned the "poetized statement" as completely non-critical and ideologically mystifying. For Plato, the kind of consciousness required for distanced, critical analysis would take the form of the dialectical method, built on the structure of hypotactic logic.[6] The most extreme form of this opposition sees parataxis, the associative style of the epic, to be incapable of containing "logical" thought (Ong 15, 40, 52–57). But, as many commentators point out, there are forms of logic in the epics other than inference based on the accumulation of incident or causation explained as the intercession of the gods (Murphy, *Synoptic* 4; Kennedy, *Rhetoric* 9; Whitman). Indeed, the very "ring structure" of the epic narrative has been laid out in the form of a logical argument by Nestle (Willcock). Thus examining the forms of logic in the speeches in the *Iliad* will provide important clues to the evolution of rationality out of a "mythic" age. More central to an understanding of the sophists, the rhetorical moments of the epic—persuasive situations and internal deliberations—supply the most concentrated examples of logic and argument within the larger narrative.

The very high degree of community agreement on the "custom-laws" (*nomoi*) contained in the epics, in Havelock's view, would seem to deny any possibility for critical perspective—for conflict of the kind rhetoric would eventually be formulated to negotiate. But, in fact, the very theme of the *Iliad* arises from just such a conflict: Achilles's anger at the violation of the gift distribution custom by Agamemnon on the ground of the latter's power of position (Nimis, "Language" 72–73). This conflict is read by Rose as foreshadowing the challenge to hereditary kingship by ability that leads to the age of tyrannies and eventually paves the way for democracy. Even if the representation of negotiation in Homer is the anachronistic imposition of a feature of a later society onto the Mycenaean setting (Havelock, *Preface* 121), the fact remains that the mythic discourse is capable of containing the beginnings of a "rhetorical consciousness" (Murphy, *Synoptic* 3–4).[7] This consciousness expresses itself both through public argument and internal debate.

Book IX of the *Iliad* stands as the most famous example of the use of persuasion in an explicitly rhetorical setting. Achilles, angry because of Agamemnon's theft of his war "prize," Briseis, refuses to take part in the battle, so Agamemnon sends an embassy of the most important and persuasive Greeks to try to convince him to return. The forms of argument we might expect to find under this culture

would emphasize "natural" authority (i.e., by birth traced to a divine
origin), combined with the threat of physical force. Another moral
imperative of Greek society was the shame attached to behavior
outside accepted mores: specifically, disobeying the father in a heavily
patriarchal social order (Dodds 15–18). Though arguments of authority and shame do appear in Book IX (Kennedy, *Rhetoric* 13–14), they
are combined with others aimed at persuading Achilles to return to
the fighting. Indeed, the most important speech, and ultimately the
only one that moves Achilles to change his course of action, uses
narrative itself as an argument. Phoenix, Achilles's old tutor and
guardian, tells a story of Meleager, who refused to fight in exchange
for gifts, but was ultimately drawn into battle without any reward.
Willcock argues that this narrative, as well as a number of others,
embodies a paradigmatic form parallel to the narrative "logic" of the
"ring structure" itself (142).[8] Whitman sees Phoenix as unwittingly
clarifying Achilles's intentions through the Meleager story (191); it
clearly persuades him not to leave, though he still refuses to fight for
Agamemnon.

How would this section of the epic have been processed by
a listener with a "preliterate" or "oral" consciousness? Given the
confrontations among competing codes of behavior in Book IX, it is
difficult to imagine that section of the poem producing the kind
of unconscious identification Havelock sees Plato protesting as the
characteristic audience response to the recitations of oral poetry.
Would the listeners perhaps be taking sides, empathizing with or
protesting silently the positions of the various speakers? Though
this question is probably unanswerable, Finnegan's speculation that
Homeric poets adjusted their materials to fit the audience and circumstances of performance suggests that the "mythic consciousness" may
not have been as homogeneous as the orality/literacy proponents
would suggest. She recommends "publication" as a more suitable
term than "transmission" for the information-exchange undertaken
by oral poetry (Finnegan 155). Willcock's discovery of the unique
forms of separate narrative "arguments" in the *Iliad* leads him to
argue that the poet was, in fact, inventing narrative details to make the
stories fit the parallel circumstances of the character to be persuaded

(Willcock 152). The degree of sensitivity to argumentative structure implied here on the part of the audience, along with the inventiveness of the poet, seems inconsistent with a picture of listeners lulled by the mechanical recital of a completely familiar tale. A more general conclusion to be drawn from these pieces of Homeric scholarship is that the "mythic" condition can not be said to exclude certain forms of "logic" later formalized, though they are not yet documented. Kirk et al. similarly note a high degree of "logical and psychological refinement . . . already present" in Odysseus's power of analysing complex circumstances (73). Could these forms of argument, even though they were not written down, have been taught as a code? Donlan argues that the sophistication and "preparation" of argument in the epics, combined with historical evidence indicating few resources for physical coercion available during the period, indicate that formal teaching of persuasive argument was quite possible, even likely during an "oral" era. He offers the scene of judicial argument represented on Achilles's shield (*Iliad* XVIII. 497–508) as further evidence for the possibility of a formal attention to rhetoric in the "mythic" age.

While public deliberation in the epic can imply certain cognitive conditions at variance with the most unqualified state of "orality," specific representations of mental activity in Homer provide more direct material for consideration. Bruno Snell's famous study, *The Discovery of Mind,* gave impetus to the division of a mythic from a rational consciousness by pointing out the absence of words equivalent to later Platonic concepts of soul and mind (8–14). Indeed, Snell's emphasis on the concrete language of Homer in contrast to the later development of abstraction through use of the neuter article (227–28) grounds Havelock's (and others') orality/literacy case. For Snell, every action in Homer, including "thought," is motivated by the gods. The human is internally at peace, unquestioning: "there are no divided feelings in Homer . . . no genuine reflexion, no dialogue of the soul with itself" (19). This absence of self-reflexivity, of the ability to think contradictory propositions and decide between them, is a cardinal feature of the oral mind for the proponents of the theory. An audience incapable of such mental operations would likewise be incapable of participating in rhetoric except as the victims of manipulation.

But since Snell's influential book, some classicists have questioned his estimation of mental activity in Homer. The *Iliad* contains a number of scenes in which a single character thinks to himself (Fenik 68–69). While Dodds (following Snell) finds that mental change occurs in the mythic consciousness through the "psychic intervention" of a divine presence (17), in none of the passages Fenik cites does a god intervene. In fact, the poet represents a kind of decision-making process through reflection, without the intercession of an external force. Snell emphasizes in such cases the separation of a part of the anatomy to stand in as an interlocutor: the hero *dielexato* (carries on a dialogue) with his *thumos*—the spirit or animus, seat of passion, enthusiasm, will or purpose (19). This substitution, then, for Snell means that the Homeric self contains no independent power of making decisions. But Russo and Simon describe this situation as one of several types of "personified interchanges" (487), represented as such and not as reflection per se because of the Homeric tendency to depict "that which is common and publicly observable" (487). Fenik, considering four such internal dialogues, discovers that the structure of argument differs in the four cases he considers; it is not completely determined by the rigid structure of oral formulae. Beginning his analysis with recent arguments that the Homeric "self" does include the capacity for choice, he shows that the four cases of reflection differ in significant ways, indicating they are not merely repetitions of a pattern. In each case, the character "articulates the dilemma in his own terms" (71), contemplating different grounds for action. Fenik concludes that the theory of oral poetry "explains only half" the stylistic complexity and character development of these scenes (90). Nor does its offshoot, an oral theory of consciousness, account for the variety of dialogic mental activity present in these scenes. This capacity for reflection on grounds for action, for contemplating and choosing from among competing options, is a necessary precondition for rhetoric—in the audience as well as the speaker. Once again, imagining such passages washing over an audience completely unaware of the cognitive tension and resolution represented through them is difficult.

Though only a small part of the *Iliad* has been considered here, this inquiry into a rhetorical logic in the narrative could be carried out in many other places. The kinds of "logic" discoverable in these narratives is, of course, filtered through our post-Aristotelian epistemic atmosphere; thus, the categories of myth and logic begin to be called into question.[9] But this is just the point for reevaluating a binary split like *mythos/logos* or orality/literacy, as well as for a sophistic rhetoric branded "magical" or "irrational" by a philosophic tradition. In classical histories where rhetoric is mentioned, it occupies a sort of boundary status between these two worlds. It is acknowledged to contribute to the rational enlightment (Solmsen; Kerferd) but usually as a stage along the way to Plato's dialectic and Aristotle's *Organon* (Lloyd, *Polarity* 169–71). After the complete formulation of logic by Aristotle, rhetoric appears to employ distorted versions of that logic used in ethically questionable ways to sway ignorant audiences with an affective power similar to that wielded by the Homeric minstrels. Discovering the boundary space wherein the sophists emerge is a process of reopening and reconsidering the two discrete worlds of myth and logic, and more specifically the judgments about the minds of the listeners on either side of the "Great Divide" between orality and literacy. That significant changes in the forms of linguistic expression were underway in the sixth and fifth centuries—a major claim of Havelock, Ong, and Goody—is indubitable. What is less clear is the complete stability of the Homeric language (Nimis, "Language") and nature of the consciousness it shaped. To the extent that this analysis of logic and mental activity in the epic has succeeded, it indicates a greater capacity for reflection and thus for response within a rhetorical, or deliberative, setting than those histories under critical examination would allow.

Democracy, *Nomos,* and Rhetoric

Another way to complicate the *mythos/logos* formulation comes through a different kind of approach to the period. Social history can supplement literary analyses, providing alternative ways of judging cognitive capabilities. In the hereditary kingships of a warrior culture, the right to speak with authority fell most often to the head of the highest-born family. In the Homeric assembly, heralds handed around a scepter to designate the right to speak during debates (e.g., I. 245–46; II. 185–86, 278–82). But even in the epic, there was competition for authority; all the warriors were "kings" of their own territories and the highest leader called on his council to help him with important decisions (M. Finley 79–83). We have just seen how the persuasive speeches in Book IX of the *Iliad* concern conflicts within one aristocratic council between warrior-kings with competing claims for priority. Evolving political organizations and the spaces they inhabited created certain forms of language use other than strict poetic recitation in the "pre-rational" centuries (Vernant 39).

Though we generally think of the democracy as a sixth-and fifth-century phenomenon, there is evidence that for centuries before, villagers, each holding under a feudal arrangement a section of land called a *damos,* met in a common space perhaps for the purpose of deciding on questions of agricultural practice or on the nature of requests to be delivered to the king and his council (Vernant 32–34). Though opportunities for speaking in these meetings may not have been equally distributed in the Mycenaean period itself, the discourse context suggests a substantially different role for the listener/participant than that of the audience for a recitation of epic verse. Ultimately, argues Vernant, the political space of these village meetings became defined as a place for negotiating between the warrior and craft or land-working classes. It was clearly not the interior of the palace but rather a "middle space," in which "those who contended with words, who opposed speech with speech, became [even] in this hierarchical society a class of equals" (Vernant 46). Out of the gradual process of democratization on several fronts—from kingship to the shared responsibility of oligarchy, from the independence of the horse warrior to the collective effort of the hoplite phalanxes—relations of equality deriving from recognition of similarity created contexts for rhetorical discourse. Against the backdrop of these social and political changes, the "mythic consciousness" must have been undergoing change. The voice of the minstrel may have become less like a voice inside one's own head (if that had ever been the case) and more like a voice to which occurred responses or questions in the mind of the listener. The development of the choral leader and communal response began to produce such exchanges in poetry. This concept of changing communal identification—from individual to group— exactly reverses the transformation of a communal consciousness into individualism. It foregrounds the perception of shared interests necessary for rhetoric to work. More generally it demonstrates that a change in consciousness can be traced to other sources than the development of literacy, with different results.

Shaping rules for local democracies engaged the Greeks in an epistemological struggle. Under the old system of aristocratic king-ship, law could ultimately be attributed to a source of authority outside of human experience: the will of the gods. Statutes them-selves, or *thesmoi*, were imposed externally. But the growing impor-tance of group deliberation in making political decisions challenged that external source of "law." The emergence of democratic reform is recorded in the abrupt replacement at the time of Cleisthenes of *thesmos* by *nomos*, denoting law "as the expression of what the people as a whole regard as a valid and binding norm" (Ostwald 55). Some reflection on the significance of *nomos*, a concept closely identified with the sophists, during the period in question may help to mark out a space for the political within the linguistic territory of the "mythic" and the "logical."

An older form of *nomos* (*nomós*) meant "pasture," but even within the Homeric epic it was used metaphorically for "a range of words" and in Pindar to mean "habitation" (Liddell and Scott, *Greek-English Lexicon* 1180). An apparently later form (the accent moves to the first syllable, but both derive from the same verb, *nemo*) completes the metaphorical transfer from pasture to habitation, signifying "habitual practice, usage, or custom." Common to both forms is the importance of human agency: in the first case, in the marking out and distributing of land; and in the second, in explicitly human ratification of norms as binding. Originally something "apportioned, distributed or dis-pensed," *nomos* came to mean something "believed in, practised or held to be right" (Guthrie, *Sophists* 55). The earliest assemblies, whose business concerned the distribution of land, grew into the councils of military advisers and finally the representative assemblies legislated by Solon's and Cleisthenes's reforms, whose functions included making decisions about a full range of social and political issues.

Thus rhetoric can be closely linked with *nomos* as a process of articulating codes, consciously designed by groups of people, opposed both to the monarchical tradition of handing down decrees and to the supposedly non-human force of divinely controlled "natural law." These definitions help to locate an understanding of *nomos* in the context of the movement from *mythos* to *logos*. If the mythic world is based on an uncritical acceptance of a tradition warranted by nature (*physis*), then a sophistic interest in *nomos* represents a challenge to that tradition (Kerferd 129–30; Dodds 183–84). If, on the other hand, *logos* in its ultimately Platonic form signifies a necessary system of discourse allowing access to certain Truth, then *nomos* stands in opposition as the possibility for reformulating human "truths" in historically and geographically specific contexts. A substitution of *nomos* for *logos* appears in Vernant's description of Solon's law as *nomos*, meaning a kind of political rationalism, "reigning in the place of the king at the center of the city" (86). In a substitution for a metaphysical *logos*, Untersteiner defines *nomos* as the human capacity to "fix the main headings of reality" by means of a "humanizing essence" (Untersteiner 59). In other words, in epistemological terms it signifies the imposition of humanly determined patterns of explanation for natural phenomena in contrast to those assumed to exist "naturally" or without the conscious intervention of human intellect. The intersection of *nomos* with *logos* in the natural philosophers will help to elaborate a reconstruction of this fluid concept as it may be applied to sophistic rhetoric.

Nomos, Logos, and Natural Philosophy

The sixth-century philosopher-poets are said to mark a turning point in the transformation from *mythos* to *logos* (Havelock, *Revolution* 220f.).[10] They could be called the first intellectuals—thinkers who sought explanations for the natural world outside of the framework of myth. On one view, they projected the concept of "law" from social and political spheres onto the natural world (Vernant 108). Rather than *mythoi* they wrote *historia:* i.e., accounts available for detached and systematic investigation (Vernant 102). Their published discourse ranged from obscure, gnomic fragments (Heraclitus) to the first prose (Anaximander), linguistic experimentations Havelock sees as crucial in the revision of "speculative systems" (*Revolution* 256). Many of the Presocratic philosophers employed meter and some may have engaged in oral performance. Though the performance situation for the natural philosophers is difficult to reconstruct, much of the work of the Presocratics may have been initially composed, as well as later distributed, in written form. But its literate form did not deny broad access to their thought.[11] Vernant interprets the appearance of sixth-century philosophic speculation about natural knowledge as a transfer not only of political and social questions but of "scientific" ones as well to the realm of public debate (51–52, 107, 120).

Though they shared the features just described, the works of the Presocratic philosophers can hardly be described more specifically in terms of common goals or philosophical orientation. Indeed, though their primary interest was the natural world, much of their work, already on the formal boundaries of the literary and the philosophical, demonstrates the rich intermixture of ideas about the physical and metaphysical, the natural and the political—a mixture characteristic of pre-Aristotelian thought. Parmenides and Pythagoras, for example, were probably influential in preparing the way for Plato's doctrine of Forms, while Zeno's paradoxes led to an extreme skepticism. The central project of the Milesians was to "name a single material from which the whole differentiated world could have grown" (Kirk et al. 162), resulting in claims that the totality of earthly matter could be reduced to water (Thales) or air (Anaximenes).

The sophists found unacceptable the essentializing gesture by which a philosopher could identify a single element and rejected the claim of order warranted by *physis*. For this reason they are frequently characterized as uninterested in natural phenomena (Guthrie, *Sophists*

15). But the sophists' debts to Heraclitus, Anaximander, Xenophanes, and Democritus indicate connections between the philosophers' physical speculations and the social/political world of rhetoric.[12] Havelock's *Liberal Temper in Greek Politics* elaborates those connections eloquently, showing finally how Plato and Aristotle distorted the physical and social theories of their liberal predecessors (including the sophists with Presocratics) to bring them into service of a conservative political agenda. But in his later work with literacy (*Preface, Revolution*), Havelock focuses almost entirely on the Presocratics' development of an abstract language suitable for fourth-century philosophy. Somehow Havelock's attempt to trace the linguistic achievement of a philosophical language came to eclipse his earlier critical approach to the evolution of political theory. Though an integration of these two Havelockian agendas is beyond the scope of this study, I will try here, through a brief look at some issues of importance in the development of sophistic rhetoric, to balance Havelock's relentless focus on progress toward rationality in the literacy work with observations from his earlier work with the sophists. The issues in question are the implications of the Presocratic's logic for narrative and their anthropological speculations.

Heraclitus is best known for his doctrine of perpetual change, an observation leading directly to the sophists' interests in social difference. He does, however, write about natural "law." He refers to the subject of his investigation as *logos,* asserting it to be common knowledge as against a "private misunderstanding." But he defines *logos* as a method of arrangement, measure, reckoning, proportion (Kirk et al. 187)—a system Guthrie ("Flux") and Kerferd describe as a dynamic explanation of change rather than a fixed cosmic law. In another fragment, Heraclitus suggests that human *nomoi* are "nourished" by the the larger organizing principle of the physical world. In drawing such a link, he creates for the first time an ethics "formally interwoven with physics" (Kirk et al. 211–12). Havelock ignores the doctrine of flux in *Temper,* later reading Heraclitus solely in terms of the orality/literacy thesis. On the one hand, he finds Heraclitus's technique of linking oppositions in an associative chain most significant as a memory device (*Revolution* 241). On the other, he concludes that Heraclitus is a "foe" of flux in Homeric speech in his attempt to create a language "timeless, nonparticular, and comprehensive" (246–47). Lloyd seems more aware of the problem of teleologically antici-pating later developments. Though Lloyd, finally, credits Aristotle with the highest development in logic, he gives Heraclitus credit for "exploit[ing] the paradoxes which result from equivocation to great effect" (*Polarity* 102). When paradox is seen as leading to the contra-dictory arguments Protagoras identified as the basis of rhetorical encounters and the only possible source of knowledge, the route to a necessary logic of non-contradiction is turned aside. There is at least a suggestion here that cognitive and linguistic development may not always have been rolling relentlessly in the direction of Aristotle—that other arrangements of thought and language were possible.

Another kind of change generated by the logical fomentation of the Presocratics concerns causality. In Homer's world, the gods were agents of natural change (Havelock, *Preface* 168–69). Their interces-sion provided simple explanations of complex causes for events such as the erosion of the wall built by the Greeks in Troy (Havelock, *Preface* 264–65). In Hesiod's mythical cosmogony, written in the century preceding the Presocratics, the arrival of a god introduced order into chaos. A temporal occurrence in the narrative served as an ordering principle. But for the first philosophers, the cause embodied in the concrete god becomes an abstract force (Havelock, *Preface* 300); a narrative event translates into an elementary principal. This metamorphosis is preserved in the philological history of the Greek word *arche,* meaning "first" or "beginning" in a concrete, temporal sense, but eventually coming to mean "law" or "principle" (Vernant 114–15). Havelock sees the invention of abstraction as a stage in the inevitable progress toward non-narrative, philosophic prose; it was necessary for narrative to give way in order for abstract thought to develop (Havelock, *Preface* 300). The appearance of causality in narrative contexts in the Presocratics, however, suggests a more com-plex, less "inevitable" relationship between narrative and logic. Anaxi-mander, for example, casts the physical process of birth and death allegorically, wherein things "pay penalty and retribution to each other for their injustice according to the assessment of Time" (Kirk et al. 118). Because together the fragments of this poet/philosopher's work offer a comprehensive and rational theory of the origins of human life, there is little chance that this narrative account represents an older mythic attribution of cause to the gods. Perhaps Anaximander found narrative a fruitful mode for natural description, a vehicle not inconsonant with the more abstract language he used in other places. A further inquiry into the possible uses for narrative in systematic explanations will be deferred to the analysis below of the actual writings of two sophists. For now, we can conclude that the relevance of the natural philosophers to the sophists can be found partly in their interest in methods of arranging language for constructing explanations of the natural world (Havelock, *Preface* 289), but hold in abeyance the conclusion that their linguistic innovations, including the introduction of abstraction, necessarily demanded a complete rejection of the "poetic" discourse of previous generations.

The sophists' experiences of widely varying cultures with different notions of "truth" offered confirmation at the level of the social of the views of Heraclitus and Empedocles, who saw a physical universe full of a multitude of varied phenomena constantly in flux (Enos, "Epistemology"). This view of nature grounded "scientifically" the pragmatic *paideia* they offered their changing society. They found sympathetic as well the anthropological theories of Anaximander and Xenophanes, whose fragmentary works explicitly deny the human relation to the gods established in the myths and replace it with evolutionary accounts of human development. For both, change is a crucial element of the physical world (Kirk et al. 162, 177), a feature which necessarily limits human knowledge (Kirk et al. 179). Democritus provides another source from which the sophists may have formulated a discourse of change. A younger contemporary of Protagoras, Democritus formulated a physical theory of atomism with ethical and political implications. For him, the world is composed of an infinite number of atoms with an inherent "tendency" to order, but ordered neither by accident nor by a transcendent force. His related view of human society posits the formation of patterns "describable in terms not of mechanical but of political behaviour" producing solutions for problems of pleasure and pain, profit and loss, and others (Havelock, *Temper* 154).

The significance of this theory for the sophists lies in the human agency for change and in the continuity between physical and social forms. It seems Havelock found little in Democritus to feed his later interest in the progress toward an abstract language; thus the absence of Democritus in the later texts. He is of significant interest, however, in understanding the development of a sophistic "epistemology." For the sophists, following Democritus, because no particular order is necessary, the argument of probability becomes the most useful both for understanding historical cause and for deciding on future action (Cole 146). The first historians, Herodotus and Thucydides, writing a generation apart in the fifth century, also drew heavily on the logic of probability. They well understood the complexities of recreating a story of the past as a process less "scientific" than rhetorical. Aristotle, of course, makes a great deal of the importance of probable arguments in rhetoric. But identifying the sources of this feature of sophistic rhetoric disentangles it from Aristotle's later system. In the *Rhetoric,* probability appears as a second-rate substitute for certainty, which is unattainable in the messy world of politics and ethics. History does not employ probability in Aristotle's view because it is only a matter of accumulating facts, which can be completely improbable; he contrasts historical discourse with the creation of poetry in which probability is desirable but not necessary. Replacing the argument from probability in an earlier epistemological world, however, shows it to be the only means of "achieving a true picture of the world" in which infinite possibilities are shaped by human action (Cole 147). Acknowledging an epistemological status for probability demands in discourse a flexible process of ordering or arranging, a feature of both *nomos* and narrative.

What I have tried to do through this overview of literary, political, and philosophical backgrounds to the sophists is complicate the historical trope dominating most historical accounts of them: the revolutionary triumph of *logos* over *mythos*. The intrusion of rhetoric into this neat progress demands a recalculation of the values of each term, reading the one in terms of the other. A creative exploration of the term *nomos* offers an alternative to the *mythos/logos* polarity— an analytical frame for redescribing sophistic discourse, ordered by a flexible narrative logic and used to construct knowledge across a range of fields. Elaborating more fully a sophistic rhetorical epistemology requires a close look at two central figures in the movement: Gorgias and Protagoras.

In most histories, the sophists are buried under the sweep of "philosophy" in its progress toward the fully "rational" mind (e.g., Havelock, *Preface* 280). Though Havelock emphasizes the complexity of the transition, sometimes he draws the lines between the mythic and logical quite clearly: "With the slow transition from verse to prose and from concrete towards abstract the man of intelligence came to represent the master of a new form of communication . . . now anti-poetic" (*Preface* 287). Under this view, the sophists fall just short of the full realization of a rational, literate consciousness because of the traces of oral, poetic language left in their persuasive discourse. From another classical perspective, the sophists represent a completely "rational" rejection of a "conglomerate of religious views" rigidly controlling behavior under a patriarchal shame culture (Dodds 188). While positioning the sophists astutely within the evolution of ethical systems, Dodds's reading denies any emotional component to the sophistic process of restructuring social control because it ignores completely their discourse practice (185). Wherever the sophists are placed on the *mythos/logos* continuum, the explanatory power of that motif has dominated their treatment. De Romilly's analysis of the technical "magic" of Gorgias provides a most sensitive understanding of a rational system of irrational rhetoric (*Magic* 16). She narrates the ultimate suppression of a self-consciously emotional rhetoric by the differently motivated magic of Socrates (36) and the completely logical *techne* of Aristotle (55). But even her careful account leaves out the political reasons why such a shift would occur. She attributes the reemergence of a magical rhetoric in the French symbolist poets in the nineteenth century to an accidental pendulum swing of preference (88). A major challenge for the historian of rhetoric in evaluating the sophists lies in the attempt to position their work within the *mythos/*

logos frame. The readings which follow seek to disentangle the artfully interwoven strands of narrative—the "mythic" mode of organization—and "rational" argument, to show a mixed discourse shaped by prose writers fully in control of both forms.

Protagoras and *Dissoi Logoi*

The oldest sophist, Protagoras of Abdera (in Thrace) probably lived from 490 to 420 B.C. (Sprague 3). His literary remains are the most fragmentary of all the figures associated with the movement, and for that reason he has received little attention from historians of rhetoric, who usually focus on Gorgias (Murphy, *Synoptic* 8–9; Kennedy, *Rhetoric* 25). But a balanced picture of the sophists demands an interpretation of Protagoras's contribution. As a close associate of Pericles, he was engaged in the democratic experiment at its height, writing laws for the colony of Thurii in 444. His fragments stand as key doctrines in sophistic thought, while his representation in two Platonic dialogues offers a fuller picture of his political and epistemological orientation and the style of his discourse.

One of the fragments of commentary about him asserts that he was the first to say that there were two contradictory arguments about everything (Sprague 21), an observation expressed by the Greek phrase *dissoi logoi*. From our location on the far side of Aristotle's insistence on the Law of Non-Contradiction, we respond readily to certain interpretations of this observation: that it provides a logical basis for opportunistically taking any side in an argument, for making the weaker case the stronger (Murphy, *Synoptic* 9); or that it represents a step along the way to Plato's later "clarification" of the problem of contradiction (Lloyd, *Polarity* 110, 113).[13] But under the epistemology attributed to Protagoras in *Theaetetus* and revealed by other fragments, *dissoi logoi* are unavoidable outcomes of any group discourse. The title of one of Protagoras's lost works, *Truth*, bears the subtitle *Refutations* (Sprague 18), suggesting that the sophist understood *dissoi logoi* to be a means of discovering *a* truth rather than the expression of a distance from a separate, single Truth within phenomena. His most famous saying reinforces this notion: "Of all things the measure is human, of the things that are, that they are, and of the things that are not, that they are not" (Sprague 18). Protagoras denies any significance to the existence of phenomena outside individual human experience. He is given the opportunity to lay out his doctrine about sensation in Plato's dialogue *Theaetetus*. The character "Protagoras" there argues that a wind that feels hot to one person and cold to another really *is* both hot and cold (151Eff).[14] The sophist found it both impossible and unnecessary to determine any single Truth about appearances; more important is negotiating useful courses of action for groups of people given their varying perceptions about the world. That understanding and use comes to be through the propositions people form about them: in other words, the human-as-measure doctrine is an answer to *dissoi logoi* (Untersteiner 49). It is important to identify the recognition of contradictory statements as a starting point for the rhetorical work of Protagoras and other sophists rather than a despairing conclusion about the futility of human inquiry, as for the Eleatics like Zeno who engaged in absurd paradoxes (Solmsen 18). Further evidence of Protagoras's rejection of any truth outside of human experience is his comment on the gods: "Concerning the gods, I am not able to say whether they exist or what they are like, for there are many things that hinder me" (Sprague 10). Though a skeptical attitude toward the gods was not uncommon in the fifth century (Kerferd 167), Protagoras's agnosticism contributes to the general picture of his knowledge theory (Guthrie, *Sophists* 234). Like the Presocratics, who sought reasons for physical phenomena outside the explanations of myth, Protagoras's careful expression of ignorance directs energy away from the search for an external knowledge source and throws the responsibility for determining the nature of things onto humans (Untersteiner 31).

While the human-as-measure doctrine offers the core of a response to the tragic condition of being trapped by contradictory propositions, a fuller explanation of what that release entails comes in the "Great Speech."[15] Despite Socrates's attempts throughout the dialogue to ruffle "Protagoras" with his hard-edged dialectic, the wise old sophist retains a kind of genial good humor, at least at this stage of the dialogue. He demonstrates his ability to read the character and needs of his audience in choosing the form of his discourse. "Once upon a time," he begins, "there were gods only, and no mortal creatures" (¶320d). As an old man among young men, he chooses an entertaining narrative over dry argumentation as the most effective way of showing that civic responsibility can indeed be taught, Socrates's objections to the contrary. Protagoras employs here parataxis, a syntactic structure characteristic of "primitive" story-telling, including the Homeric epic poems. Free from the tighter bonds of its "logical" alternative, the loose association of clauses without hierarchical connectives or embedding is considered to be a less sophisticated organization than hypotaxis, the highest expression of which is Aristotelian propositional logic. Parataxis creates a distinctive character in an age when Homeric myth has lost its social force and rhapsodes hold a questionable status (Enos, "Rhapsode"). Though "Protagoras" uses the familiar formula of the story-teller, the effect of this myth is not the hypnotic mystification to which Plato objected in the oral poetry of his fathers (Havelock, *Preface*) but rather myth as "externalized thought" (Untersteiner 58): a narrative offering a provisional explanation of a human condition through time. "Protagoras" blurs the line between *mythos* and *logos,* spinning off moral arguments from straightforward narrative. These are not the repeated maxims and lessons of customary behavior learned through the oral tradition, but rather *new* solutions to the problems of social organization posed by democracy. The transition from story to its application demonstrates its use.[16] After Zeus has distributed the qualities of justice and mutual respect to early humans equally, they are able to form cities:

> And this is the reason, Socrates, why the Athenians, and humankind in general, when the question relates to excellence in carpentry or any other mechanical art, allow but a few to share in their deliberations. And when anyone else interferes, then as you say, they object if he be not of the few; which, as I reply, is very natural. But when they meet to deliberate about political excellence or virtue, which proceeds only by way of justice and self-control, they are patient enough of any man who speaks of them, as is also natural, because

they think that every man ought to share in this sort of virtue, and that states could not exist if this were otherwise. I have explained to you, Socrates, the reason of this phenomenon. (¶322d–323a)

The sophist combines narrative with rhetorical argument to make his case.

Another kind of analysis of *logos* applied to "Protagoras" finds him falling short of Plato's Socrates in his ability to engage in dialectic (Taylor 76). The failure of the sophist to compete successfully with Socrates in his contest of dialectical reasoning can be taken as a way to position rhetoric in subordination to the newly developing logic of the fourth century. Rhetoric, as Socrates complains to "Protagoras," consists of long speeches (¶334d, ¶338a) that befuddle the listeners, perhaps in the same manner as the epic recitations of past centuries (¶315a). On this point, Havelock provides an extensive defense of Protagorian rhetoric (though he will not call it that) as generating a kind of critical mental activity (*Temper* 191–230). Unlike Kennedy, who finds "sophistic rhetoric" focused on the speaker, Havelock argues that in the sophists' work "we are invited to keep our eye not upon the authoritarian leader, but upon the average man as citizen of this society and voter in his parliament" (*Temper* 230). Sophistic rhetoric is to be understood "not as the practice of unscrupulous persuasion upon the blind emotions of masses . . . but those complex processes and subtle currents of judgment which go to the making of the collective mind and the group decision" (*Temper* 230). In Havelock's view, sophistic rhetorical practice was not "confused until made to appear so by the use of formal logic," but rather flexible and complex (201). He spells out its foundations, which "stand the Platonic convictions on their head" (201).

When Havelock imagines a kind of dialogue going on in the minds of participants in the assemblies during the course of an oral argument (*Temper* 223), he creates a far different picture from the cognitive state of audiences under the earlier condition of "orality." The term *logos,* it seems, is in the case of the sophist inadequate to describe a complex form of communication under which "organized discourse present[s] ideas and channel[s] emotions . . . bearing on common affairs" (*Temper* 192). The expression *nomos*, suggested earlier as a potential alternative to *mythos* and *logos*, suggests something of this process in its etymology. On the level of the social, *nomos* determines the behavior and activities of persons and things through convention. In its relation to a cognate verb meaning "think," it suggests a mental process of acceptance or approval (Kerferd 112). Indeed, in its coalescence of the public and the private, the term can be taken to signify a characteristic rhetorical condition of language use. While *nomos* "presupposes an acting subject—believer, practitioner or apportioner—a mind" (Guthrie, *Sophists* 55), so does it demand a social context in which to take effect. In appropriating the term for a mode of linguistic activity, that fusion of public and private becomes a feature of the process of distributing or ordering arguments. Through an imaginative extension, we could call "Protagoras" himself a kind of Promethean creator, ordering a story of the world for his audience in the "Great Speech." His "distribution" of ideas, self-conscious in its blend of *mythos* and *logos*, finally builds an argument for a democratic social structure, one whose job is the continual renegotiation of *nomoi* through rhetoric.

Gorgias and the Necessity of *Apate*

Gorgias of Leontini (in Sicily) lived over a century, from 490 to 380 B.C. Though he is known to have been a successful teacher and speaker, his extant works leave a perplexing picture of his enterprise. In a philosophical treatise surviving in outline and two epideictic orations (Sprague 42–67), the sophist seems to be engaging in absurd or futile goals. His treatise, *On the Nonexistent*, seen as parody by some (Guthrie, *Sophists* 193–94) or at least as not serious (Freeman 362), argues that nothing exists, or if it exists it cannot be known, or if it is known, it cannot be communicated. In the only extant orations, he chooses to defend traitors, one the infamous mythical Helen of Troy. Gorgias is perhaps most famous for his antithetical style, said to have left audiences confused and even spellbound by its elaborateness. The composite picture suggests to some a "philosophical nihilist" (Enos, "Epistemology" 46 n. 55): a skeptic bent on demonstrating, often perversely, the antisocial potential for persuasive language given such an epistemological condition.

But Gorgias served as an effective diplomat and was a highly successful teacher. How do we reconcile the apparent message of his fragments with his life work as a rhetor? The answer to that question begins with Gorgias's speculations on language. Of primary interest in all of the texts is the gap between word and thing. In *On the Nonexistent,* he asserts that "*logos* is not evocative of the external" (Sprague 46). Palamedes, in his *Defense,* argues that it is not possible for words to bring the truth of past actions before the jury without doubt (Sprague 62). Not only in law but in natural philosophy does that gap operate: astronomers, for example, can remove one opinion and plant another, to "make what is incredible and unclear seem true to the eyes of opinion" (Sprague 53). One reading of this language theory leads to the Platonic conclusion that this gap is a bad thing and needs to be closed—that language fails unless it is seamlessly congruent with the phenomenal world. Despite the epistemic shift underway since Nietzsche redefined "lies," the Platonic reading still has some currency.

Gorgias himself identified possibly dangerous effects of a language that cannot be trusted to represent perfectly the material world. Opinion created by language can be "a most untrustworthy thing" (Sprague 60); speeches can, like a drug, "bewitch the soul with a kind of evil persuasion" (Sprague 53). But like some drugs, *logos* can also bring good effects, saving life and causing delight. Indeed, the *Encomium of Helen* is largely a meditation on the awesome *logos,* "a powerful lord, which by means of the finest and most invisible body effects the divinest works" (Sprague 52). Gorgias's project was in part to understand how that complex relationship worked. Despite those potential abuses, there was for the sophists no possibility of language providing complete access to the Truth; opinion is all citizens have to go on in making decisions. Though opinion is never based securely on knowledge of the phenomenal, Gorgias does identify a relation between the two: "existence is not manifest if it does not involve opinion, and opinion is unreliable if it does not involve existence" (Sprague 66). Language plays a role in both these operations: "being" only becomes recognizable through *logos,* but the opinions created by *logos* rely in part on the phenomenal. Though Gorgias anticipated the linguistic/philosophical revolution of Nietzsche, Saussure, and Derrida, he didn't go quite so far as to locate all meaning in language. For Gorgias, externals have a role in creating the language we form through visual perception. Impressed with the inaccessibility of that non-verbal, real world, he reminds us that what we see has its own nature, not chosen by us (Sprague 46): "sight engraves upon the mind images of things which have been seen. And many frightening impressions linger, and what lingers is exactly analogous to [what is] spoken" (Sprague 54). The common denominator between visual reception and verbal expression is emotional effect (Segal).

The issue of the public function of the orator remains unanswered as yet by this theory of individual perception and language production. Despite the radical propositions of *On the Nonexistent,* often taken to lead to complete solipsism, Gorgias does not deny any possibility for communication. The point is that being itself cannot be communicated, but rather *logos* is what we communicate "to our neighbors" (Sprague 46). The internal process of both visual and verbal reception spelled out through the three texts leads ultimately to persuasion of both individuals *and* groups, the "psyche [being] the common denominator in both the collective and individual situations" (Segal 108). Gorgias, in other words, recognizes and inquires into the psychological conditions of assent for the individual who participates in the rhetorical scene of democracy. In choosing Helen to exonerate from blame, he suggests that the private, internal process of granting assent to the deceptions of language can have a public impact. Further, this process is not guided by the "rational" intellect. In his story of Helen's abduction, language is parallel with forces of violence, love, and fate, all of which exceed the bounds of rational containment. Gorgias calls that emotional experience in the space between reality and language "deception" (*apate*).

Though once again a Platonic concept of commensurability between word and thing will interpret this term pejoratively, Gorgias empties it of its moral charge, like Nietzsche in his redefinition of "lies." The sophist finds that in the creation of tragedy, "the deceiver is more honest than the non-deceiver, and the deceived is wiser than the non-deceived" (23). To understand a non-pejorative deception, we can turn to Rosenmeyer's interpretation of *logos* in Heraclitus. Whereas a philosopher like Parmenides finds a "true" formulation of reality in the speech of a master poet or philosopher (229), for Heraclitus some *logoi* are by nature ambiguous, expressed through a process of becoming, a tension working itself out in the sentence rather than the single word linked in perfect identity to the single thing. Rosenmeyer argues that Gorgias, in a "radical departure," "in a sense . . . completes Heraclitus" (230–31). Instead of a special form of speech signifying the ambiguous nature of certain realities, as for Heraclitus, *logos* is for Gorgias the only kind of speech possible, necessarily an *apate*. Though Gorgias refers explicitly to tragedy, his language theory indicates no place for a different kind of linguistic epistemology in another genre. Deception is a function of any discourse event. Rosenmeyer points out the close relationship between tragedy and rhetoric in the fifth century (235) and the continuity of the lyric poets, the Presocratic philosophers, and the sophists (238) over several centuries. No significant distinctions can divide genres as we see them today, after Aristotle, given the epistemological position of language for Gorgias. Rosenmeyer writes of the "emancipation of literature" in the fifth century, explaining a return of myth at the moment of the enlightenment as an outcome of the linguistic theories of Heraclitus and Gorgias (233–34). The positive value Gorgias assigns to "deception" draws attention to the importance of the audience's reception of a discursive performance; their mental participation and, eventually, their assent is required for any discourse to have the force of knowledge.

At this point, we can see that the *logos* Gorgias explores is quite a different concept from the rational structure of reasoning built by Plato and Aristotle. The psyche has not yet been divided into rational and "irrational" realms, as in Plato (Segal 106–08); thus *logos* stands as a holistic process of verbal creation and reception in Gorgias's work. This *logos* may seem to have more in common with the mythic consciousness as described by the orality/literacy scholars than with a literate rationality. Indeed, the magical, incantatory power of Gorgian rhetoric has received careful attention from de Romilly, among others. But her conclusion, that Gorgias's magic derives from the rational control of a *techne,* places the producer if not the audience of the discourse in a self-conscious relation to it (*Magic* 16), unlike the situation described by Havelock for bards in the oral tradition who had little conscious control over the contents of their recitations. Given this control, in order for Gorgias's rhetoric to escape the accusation of amoral manipulation, it would need to bring the conditions under which persuasion was effected before the audience itself as a subject for consideration. In the *Encomium of Helen,* Gorgias engages in just such a public exploration of the power of *logos*—a force coming to be seen in the mid-fifth century Greek *polis* as rivaling the fate of the gods or even physical violence in its power.[17] Thus Helen "against her will, might have come under the influence of speech, just as if ravished by the force of the mighty" (Sprague 52). Though *logos* lacks the power of fate, it takes the same form, "constraining the soul . . . both to believe the things said and to approve the things done." Though the Greek is indeed enchanting in its "poetic" effects (the Hadas translation quoted in Murphy, *Synoptic* 11, gives an especially effective English equivalent), Gorgias's topic would hardly be a prudent one for an immoral word-magician, intent on fooling people with his mesmerizing oratory. Though Gorgias was certainly alerting citizens to the power of language and ways it can be used on the unsuspecting, the well-structured argument of his own discourse balances the mesmerizing effects of his style (Swearingen, "Literate" 149). In this performance piece, linguistic speculation emerges within a narrative reevaluation of a mythic event. While in Protagoras, the distance between word and world—*dissoi logoi*—was countered by paratactic narrative in the "Great Speech," Gorgias balances the disturbing recognition of linguistic indeterminacy with the familiarity of myth, both occurring within a clearly structured argument.

While Gorgias's treatment of Helen will receive close attention in the next chapter, the mythic subject matter of his other complete work, the *Defense of Palamedes* offers equally rich opportunities for interpretation. In the mythic tradition, the defendant Palamedes was responsible with Cadmus for the invention of letters, and, like his accuser Odysseus, is referred to as "clever" and "cunning." These two features associate him with the sophists. The treason for which he is on trial in Gorgias's speech was fabricated by Odysseus, appropriately enough through the evidence of a forged letter, because Palamedes uncovered the Ithacan king's trick for escaping service in Troy (Cary et al. 638). Odysseus pretended to be crazy by sowing his fields with salt so as not to have to go with Agamemnon and Meneleus to win back Helen. Palamedes forced him to reveal his trick by throwing Odysseus's infant son Telemachus in front of the plow. Though Odysseus demonstrates his own abilities as a speaker on occasion and is even referred to with Palamedes in *Phaedrus* as author of an "art" of rhetoric (¶261b), two appearances in the literature set him specifically against the kind of public discourse advocated by the sophists.

In the *Iliad*, Odysseus reacts ferociously when the ugly Thersites takes the scepter to speak in favor of Achilles (II. 211–77). The more prestigious Ithacan beats the "fluent orator" with the very scepter symbolizing power to speak, guaranteeing that he "will not lift up [his] mouth to argue with princes" (II. 250). Odysseus aligns himself here with the privilege of hereditary kingship and shuts down the kind of political decision-making discourse which Gorgias and the other sophists made possible (Rose, "Thersites"). In the second example, from Sophocles's *Philoctetes,* Odysseus appears in an ambiguous relation to the sophists. He undertakes the education of a noble youth to serve the interests of the community—in this case, the Greek army. But a careful reading of the kinds of survival and interest represented in the play reveals that Odysseus, by encouraging manipulative and deceitful behaviour in his student, purveys a violent and selfish distortion of sophistic doctrine (Rose, *"Philoctetes"* 83). Over against the "humane enlightment" of an anthropologically grounded sophistic social theory, Odysseus represents violent self-interest (93). Gorgias has chosen, then, to articulate a defense for Palamedes against an accuser who appears in epic and contemporary sources as antagonistic to the benign aims of sophistic education and public speaking. With the anti-sophistic character of Palamedes's antagonist Odysseus sketched in, Palamedes's arguments seem much stronger; he serves as an ethical example of making the weaker case the stronger. Similarly with Helen, envisioning a real woman in her situation and historical moment under the pressure of a forced abduction gives weight to the arguments for a range of probable causes. Rather than demonstrating merely the "effrontery" necessary to argue "the most unpromising case" (Guthrie, *Sophists* 42), Gorgias, in the two epideictic speeches, seems more interested in exploring how probable arguments can cast doubt on conventional truths. His elaborate stylistic techniques must have been particularly effective in wrenching the characters out of the well-worn fabric of the epic heritage. Preferring epideixis to "straight" history (as far as we can tell from the extant fragments), Gorgias exploits the latitude offered by a rhetorical performance to combine narrative and argument toward the task of reinterpreting the mythic tradition for current social and political needs.

Gorgias's two occasional pieces, like Protagoras's speech, ruffle the smooth flow of history from *mythos* to *logos*. Laying out a number of causes for a past event in a quasi-literary form is taken as the occasion for exploring issues of vital importance for the present and future of the individual in the *polis* and for the state itself. References to *nomos* in his fragments, however, do suggest his interest in the social construction of proper behavior (Ostwald 26). Both epideictic pieces entail transgressions of such codes: Paris violates the very important guest/host relationship by stealing Helen, and Odysseus blatantly breaks the law by forging and lying about Palamedes's treachery. Disturbed by *anomia*, Gorgias does warn against the dangers of asocial, individual lawlessness (Ostwald 85). Despite the complicated workings of a holistic *logos* in the individual and group psyche—or perhaps because of that complex process—Gorgias by implication asserts the importance of a principled commitment to *nomoi*.

Locating the Sophists Between *Mythos* and *Logos*

This reassessment of the shift from an "oral" consciousness to full "rationality" by way of the sophists suggests a complication of that historical formula. Both the denial of "logical" cognitive resources for language users in preliterate centuries and the inevitability of the eclipse of narrative as a mode of cultural communication are cast into question. At the intersection of those doubts appears rhetoric, both as the vehicle for analyzing logical argument in the epic and for preserving the function of narrative in a "rational" era. While the analysis of argument in the *Iliad* has perhaps cast a shadow of doubt on the validity of an "oral consciousness" incapable of reflection or formal logic, the rereadings of the sophists' mixed discourses have demonstrated some possibilities for narrative in a rational era.

With the sophists, *nomos,* a self-conscious arrangement of discourse to create politically and socially significant knowledge, enters as a middle term between *mythos* and *logos.* This addition to classical rhetorical terminology might be used to displace the Aristotelian focus on rhetorical arguments with heightened attention to narrative structure, changing dramatically the status of arrangement and collapsing the discrete categories of *logos* and *pathos. Nomos* in its most comprehensive meaning stands for order, valid and binding on those who fall under its jurisdiction; thus it is always a social construct with ethical dimensions (Ostwald 20). It is a belief, opinion, point of view, or intellectual attitude distinguished from transcendent "truth" (Ostwald 37–38). As a concept of arrangement, *nomos* does not anticipate Plato's organic form, growing from inside; rather, it is a human invention. Like Prometheus, or his later incarnation, Frankenstein, the storyteller/rhetorician stitches together the parts. But unlike the hypnotic bard and his mesmerized audience, the composer and his co-creators, the audience, are fully aware of the craft, its potentially volatile effects, and its ultimate importance, both in defining knowledge for the group and leading them toward wise action.

The application of this reassessment of the orality/literacy thesis to current composition studies would cast serious doubt on the assumption that social groups who rely heavily on oral language forms are trapped in some sort of limited consciousness. Analysis of such language use, starting from the premise that they embody the *nomoi* of the group which generates them, would seek to discover the political force of arrangement, especially given the usually lower status of so-called "oral" language users in a highly literate dominant culture. Further, such an application would suggest an approach to "logical" forms of discourse which explores their appeal to their audiences on an affective level.

These issues concern not only ethnic minorities but also women, whose placement in the world of dominant discourse has been described on certain occasions on the basis of a falling away from standards of logic, rationality, or "clear thinking" (see Belenky et al.). The next chapter will take up the question of what the sophists might have to contribute to a dialogue about gender and discourse, first at a theoretical level and then in terms of writing and reading practices.

3

Forthwith the famous Lame God moulded clay in the
likeness of a modest maid, as the son of Cronos
purposed. And the goddess bright-eyed Athene girded
and clothed her, and the divine Graces and queenly
Persuasion put necklaces of gold upon her, and the
rich-haired Hours crowned her head with spring
flowers. And Pallas Athene bedecked her form with all
manner of finery. Also the Guide, the Slayer of Argus,
contrived within her lies and crafty words and a
deceitful nature at the will of loud thundering Zeus,
and the Herald of the gods put speech in her. And he
called this woman Pandora, because all they who dwelt
on Olympus gave each a gift, a plague to men
who eat bread.

Hesiod, *Works and Days* (69–82)

THE FIRST SOPHISTS AND
FEMINISM: DISCOURSES
OF THE "OTHER"

FEMINISM has recently begun to touch the field of rhetoric and composition with a predictable outcome: a recognition that the canon in history of rhetoric, as in the rest of the European intellectual tradition, excludes women. Another early exclusion *within* the history of rhetoric became ultimately the exclusion *of* rhetoric: i.e., the condemnation of the rhetoric of the first sophists by Plato and Aristotle, who redefine rhetoric in their own terms and subordinate it to philosophy. Thus a group of teachers and performers who were the first to formalize rhetoric as an art are largely ignored in traditional histories of rhetoric. My attempt in this chapter will be to investigate the possibility that those two exclusions—of women and of sophists—may be related and to question the uses to which that relation could be pursued both for feminism and for studies in the history of rhetoric.

First, a disclaimer: this will not be a comparison between historical sophists and real women in fifth-century B.C. Athens. There can be no doubt that material reality for women in Greek antiquity was oppressive, and that, relatively speaking, the first sophists were privileged by their gender, if not through full citizenship.[1] But even when actual physical danger was not a threat, the first sophists were assaulted by Socrates in an intellectual battle taken up with a vengeance by his student Plato—a battle with far-reaching social and political consequences. That process of intellectual marginalization will be our concern at the outset. As we have seen in previous chapters, the sophists' teaching and political practice was based on a materialist anthropology completely antithetical to metaphysics and the hierarchical epistemological structures it engenders, as well as

63

to oligarchic political theory. Drawing on evolutionary theories of human origins and development, the sophists argued for the most diverse range of human potentialities capable of cultivation by society, for which process public discourse, including the teaching of civic virtue, was essential. These views were very threatening to an elitist like Plato. Never at ease with the democracy, he laid out a stratified social order in which classes and roles were rigidly defined and power was reserved for the few. Under his system, rhetoric followed after dialectic as a science of discovering the nature of the soul upon which a speech will act (*Phaedrus* ¶60–67). For Plato, rhetoric was the means of delivering truth already discovered through dialectic; whereas, for the sophists, human perception and discourse were the only measure of truths, all of which are contingent. Though Plato provided a place for women in his ideal republic, and despite the fact that women of course were oppressed well before the fifth century, the philosophical edifice built by Plato and his student Aristotle has provided a *conceptual* ground for centuries' more exclusions.[2] Aristotle, while offering an elaborate theory of rhetoric, kept it in place as an imperfect system of reasoning, subordinate to science and dialectic (*Metaphysics,* I.1– 2). This very process of rank ordering knowledge carries gender implications. As Cixous reads it, "Organization by hierarchy makes all conceptual organization subject to man" (64).[3] DuBois, likewise, associates current gender oppositions—specifically Freudian descriptions of the male and female psyche—with the binary logic of philosophy: "We must see that this description of difference is just one more transformation of a centuries-old binarism, one consistent with the metaphysical tradition of Western philosophy" (9).[4] I will turn now to deconstruction as a method for tracing a part of that process of intellectual marginalization through which the sophists take on a striking similarity to a discursive construct of woman.

Sophist and Woman as Discursive Constructs

On the Derridian reading of Western philosophy, control in discourse is hierarchical, gained by the displacement of a degraded "other" in favor of a polar opposite. The congruence of logo- and phallocentrism places both sophistic rhetoric and woman at the negative pole against philosophy and man. Indeed, Plato and Aristotle defined philosophy through the exclusion of rhetoric as the degraded term.[5] For Plato, the sophists signified opinion as opposed to Truth, the materiality of the body (e.g., in association with cooking and cosmetics) vs. soul, practical knowledge vs. science, the temporal vs. the eternal, writing (explicitly as an artificial aid to memory) vs. speech (as the vehicle of intuited knowledge). This cluster of terms coincides on many counts with the cultural stereotype of the "feminine" operative in the West for centuries.[6] The second wave of feminism, beginning with de Beauvoir's *The Second Sex,* has exposed this gendered discourse of privilege, a process Gayatri Spivak has called "the production of a discourse of man through a certain metaphor of woman" ("Displacement" 169). The character projected onto the feminine as "other" shares with Plato's sophists qualities of irrationality (or non-rationality), magical or hypnotic power, subjectivity, emotional sensitivity; all these are devalued in favor of their "masculine" or philosophic opposites—rationality, objectivity, detachment and so on.

This parallel can be traced even more closely into the realm of "style," both as it refers specifically to language and in its more general reference to gesture, appearance, and dress. The devaluation of both the sophists and women operates as their reduction to a "style" devoid of substance.[7] Both rhetoric and women are trivialized by identification with sensuality, costume, and color—all of which are supposed to be manipulated in attempts to persuade through deception. The Greek goddess of persuasion, *Peitho,* is linked with marriage goddesses—not for her domestic skill but because of her seductive powers and trickery. Gorgias in particular was credited with the ability to hypnotize and deceive audiences through his enchanting style of oral performance. Plato's dialogue about him makes these parallels even more explicit. In it, Socrates compares rhetoric with cookery as opposed to medicine and with cosmetic arts against gymnastic exercise: in both cases, the first term describes only a knack based on collected experience and catering only to superficial desire rather than a scientific process of diagnosing and treating real needs (*Gorgias* ¶465).

The overlap of sophistic rhetoric and the "metaphor of woman" is not complete. A notable difference is the agonistic nature of the sophists as against the passivity attributed to women. But the number of similarities, I believe, suggests the possibility of tracing their parallel fates through history. Though it is impossible to generalize about discourse in all the centuries since the sophists, it can be said that the suppression of difference crucial to the operation of philosophy has often relegated the heterogeneity of sophistic discourse to the margins of the serious public work of knowledge formation and communication; the exclusion of women from these processes has often been defended in the same terms (e.g., as an absence of "rationality"). This suppression of sophistic rhetoric might be traced in the Christian search for God's truth or in the medieval emphasis on dialectic over "grammar" (i.e., poetics) and rhetoric in the trivium. The most powerful occasion of this suppression, still operative today, comes with the relegation of rhetoric by seventeenth-century science to external "color" or supplemental "dress"—meaning distorting obfuscation. The parallel oppression of women within those same intellectual systems is too well known, and too vast, to catalogue here.

Exposing Exclusions: Rhetoric, Deconstruction, Feminism

The work of bringing to light these parallel displacements has gone on under the names of rhetoric in Nietzsche (Blair), of poststructuralist theory, which also claims Nietzsche as a forerunner, and of feminism. Derrida's *Spurs,* a deconstructive analysis of the status of "woman" in Nietzsche, marks a provocative intersection of these three discourses. Derrida finds in Nietzsche three alternative positions for "woman" (97), identifications corresponding suggestively with historical positions on rhetoric. For Nietzsche, Derrida observes, woman is the figure of falsehood; we see rhetoric holding the same place for Plato. Second, for Nietzsche, woman is a handler of truth, and as such still at a distance from truth. Rhetoric functions similarly in Bacon (146). Third, Nietzsche affirms woman in herself as a power for overthrowing philosophic, hierarchical Truth. In his own work on rhetoric, Nietzsche attributes to it the same capacity for overturning Truth (Blair 106–07). Has Derrida, then, in this reading of Nietzsche, "feminized" philosophy (Spivak, "Displacement" 184) in such a way as to undo the exclusions of woman and the sophistic earlier outlined? And does rhetoric line up with "woman" as the instrument of deconstruction?

While recognizing the value of deconstructive critique for demystifying the binary structures on which the discursive power of patriarchy is built, many feminists have sought to move outside the realm of undecidability circumscribed by deconstruction (Alcoff; Poovey). In other words, they question how far deconstruction can go toward the third, affirmative role Derrida extracts from Nietzsche. Spivak warns that the "woman" whose displacement is recognized in Derridean deconstruction is not the real women whose bodies are subject to codes of legitimacy and inheritance. Thus, she asserts, women are doubly displaced in deconstruction. She uses a dual sense of *logos* to mark the difference between a textual exercise and the engagement in an investigation of material conditions of textual production. In the first sense, the *logos* to be deconstructed is the founding principal of transcendence, presence, idea, speech. But in another use of the term, *logoi* are "laws in the normal sense," creating conditions under which humans in social organizations live and write (184). "Woman" is oppressed by the former, but women suffer under the latter. Her point is that the historical and social operation of the sexual differential exceeds the discursive identification of such sexual differences. Rhetoric historically has taken as its province the analysis of those discursive acts with which Spivak is concerned. For feminists, then, committed to extending the "otherness" of "woman" to take in multiple differences of women in real material situations, "rhetoric" as the "other" of philosophy has a role in specifying real material situations of discourse performance. This common interest in historical situation suggests a fruitful intersection of rhetoric with feminism in a theoretical dialogue extending beyond a shared status as "other" within the discourse of philosophy. In two recent analyses of this problem, I find feminists turning to rhetorical possibilities as a means of understanding different directions in feminism.

Feminisms and Deconstruction

Both Toril Moi and Linda Alcoff, concerned with the limitations of particular theoretical positions, outline conflicting stages or stances in feminist politics and theory. Moi describes first a discourse of equality—an assertion that women are like men and thus deserve equal treatment (5). Alcoff does not focus on this stage, but it emerges by implication in her discussion as liberal feminism. Despite the acknowledged usefulness and necessity of arguing for equality, a feminism sensitive to the results of historical inequalities valorizes women as they are, i.e., different. Thus develops stage two, a discourse of difference (Moi 5). Alcoff calls this approach "cultural feminism" and offers the work of Mary Daly as its most typical expression.[8] If, in my initial comparison of the sophists and "woman," I had claimed an inherent value to the sophists' and women's style based only on their difference from the philosophers' regimented reasoning, my analysis could have been entered as an example of this kind of feminism. But both Moi and Alcoff explain how a feminism based on difference ultimately founders on the problem of essentialism; reinforcing difference leaves open the possibility of reproducing patriarchal exclusions (Moi 6; Alcoff 413–14). Both Moi and Alcoff find in poststructuralism a resolution for the discourse of difference, but its anti-foundational premises undercut any epistemological or linguistic fixity. This undecidability leaves no room for political struggle (Alcoff 417–22). Through poststructuralism, we lose the bases of the two previous feminisms—universal human essence or essential sexual difference—which have historically provided the grounds of political action for women (Moi 6). Moi's further discussion of post-feminism in Alice Jardine's *Gynesis* summarizes a style of reading which would attempt to give the deconstructive analysis a more positive role: valorizing and affirming "otherness" as "the feminine" wherever it appears (11–12). And in fact, this could be one way of reading the sophists back into the history of rhetoric; their difference from philosophy could simply be named "feminine" and valued as such.

But the problem troubling Moi here is the one that troubles Spivak in Derrida's text: i.e., what is the relationship between a "feminine other" and "real" women? Is the identification of the "other" in any text necessarily a feminist reading? Moi questions the easy move in which any "other" is equated with "woman," or— even trickier—with women. She argues that such readings are not automatically "feminist," but can only "produce emancipatory effects . . . [when] placed in an anti-patriarchal context" (12). In other words, the political effect of any such reading is contingent on the rhetorical situation, including the sex of the speaker and audience. By this criterion, the sophists in their own time can be taken as feminist only by implication. While their texts characterize women in potentially liberating ways (Gorgias rescues Helen; Protagoras omits Pandora), neither the texts nor the doxographical accounts provide any evidence that the male sophists sought political or social change for real women in a culture which, like our own, distributes power unequally on the basis of gender. Spivak makes a similar point when she finds deconstruction as a "feminist" practice "caught on the other side of sexual difference" ("Displacement," 184). Historical women, in fact, stand as a limit to deconstruction (184); likewise, they limit a reading of sophistic rhetoric in its historical moment as "feminist" based simply on its "otherness."

Rhetorical Feminism

Moi, Alcoff, and Spivak all work their way out of this deconstructive dilemma through strategies I would identify with sophistic rhetoric. For Moi, the three positions she sets out are incompatible and irreconcilable, but, she asserts, they must continue to coexist in contradiction. Each individual must agonistically take sides with the full knowledge that any position involves unpalatable political choices, acts of exclusion. Moi acknowledges the limits of human agency but grants that some choice is possible. What she describes are rhetorical stances. This solution is particularly resonant with sophistic rhetoric because of the sophists' emphasis on *dissoi logoi*—contradictory prop-ositions—as the anti-foundation of any knowledge (Guthrie, *Sophists* 176–225; Kerferd 59–67). The obligation of the responsible citizen, both for the first sophists and for some feminists, is the choice of a position, in full knowledge that the "economy" of her selection leaves out other, less usable truths. Alcoff offers "positionality" as an alterna-tive to cultural feminism and poststructuralism: a construction of subjectivity as historicized experience (431). She first describes the subject as a complex of concrete habits, practices, and discourses. Then she names gender as a position from which to act politically, while at the same time rejecting a universal, ahistorical definition of gender. Her label for this process is "identity politics." Though women's identities are constructed by a position in an existing cultural and social network, Alcoff denies that the concept of "woman" is determined solely by external elements:

> Rather, she herself is part of the historicized, fluid movement, and
> she therefore actively contributes to the context within which her po-
> sition can be delineated . . . the identity of a woman is the product
> of her own interpretation and reconstruction of her history, as medi-
> ated through the cultural discursive context to which she has access.
> (434)[9]

An emphasis on habit and practice, on historical contingency, and the rejection of essence all characterize the rhetoric of the sophists. Spivak as well, I would say, refers to the imperative of rhetoric to formulate kairotic discourse—i.e., suitable for the time. She advises "strategic 'misreadings'—useful and scrupulous fake readings" ("Dis-placement" 186). These descriptions baldly renounce the possibility of "true" readings and of a fixed subject, just as the sophists did. Carefully avoiding the assertion of a sovereign subject, Spivak none-theless calls on feminists to shift "woman" from the (grammatical) object of the question "What is woman?" to the position of ques-tioning subject by asking "What is man that the itinerary of his desire creates such a text?" (i.e., the text of Western phallogocentric philosophy.) Her question calls for a reconstruction of history and suggests the potential for linking feminist reading practices to the history of rhetoric.

The Case of Cixous

As a case in point, the criterion of rhetorical exigency can be applied to Cixous's discourse of difference against the charge of essentialism sometimes leveled at her self-conscious practice of women's writing. This case will return us at the same time to the question of style and then bring us back to the writing of history. The similarities of Cixous's discourse to the sophistic style are striking (and mark the beginning point of my interest in this subject). They both celebrate sensual pleasure in the sounds of words, antithesis, storytelling, poetic effects in prose forms—in fact, both playfully disrupt Aristotelian laws of genre. While Cixous's labeling of this style as "women's writing" opens her to the charge of reproducing a difference patriarchy uses to its own advantage, I would like to argue that the way she situates her practice rhetorically—i.e., within a cultural, political, historical context—tempers the charge. Cixous describes women's writing as *bisexual,* partaking in the heterogeneity of bisexuality. Right now, she says, it is only women who are capable of such a performance:

> For historical reasons, at the present time it is woman who benefits from and opens up within this bisexuality beside itself, which does not annihilate differences but cheers them on, pursues them, adds more: in a certain way *woman is bisexual*—man having been trained to aim for glorious phallic monosexuality. (85, emphasis in original)

Because she envisions a possible future in which difference is not tied ontologically to sex, her practice can be described as strategic rather than essentialist. She announces that such writing inevitably comes from within hegemonic discourse at this moment in history and attempts to undo it in an act of resistance and subversion. Cixous simultaneously performs and argues for her practice:

> If woman has always functioned 'within' man's discourse, . . . now it is time for her to displace this 'within,' explode it, overturn it, grab

> it, make it hers. . . . break[ing] with explanation, interpretations, and
> all the authorities. . . . She forgets. She proceeds by lapse and
> bounds, . . . scrambling spatial order, breaking in, emptying struc-
> tures, punching holes in the system of couples and positions, and
> with a transgression screw[s] up whatever is successive, chain-linked,
> the fence of circumfusion. (95–97)

Like Cixous's disruption of logical discourse, the sophists' uses of antithesis and fondness for contradictory arguments, along with their propensity for poetry's loosely connected narrative syntax in prose, seemed to challenge the philosophers Plato and Aristotle with a threatening disorder. They condemned the sophistic "style" for a range of features that, in fact, together sketch a profile of an alternative epistemic field: generic diversity, loose organization, a reliance on narrative, physical pleasure in language production and reception, a holistic psychology of communication, and an emphasis on the aural relation between speaker and listener. These features stand over against qualities of a patriarchal, philosophic discourse prepared (though not practiced) by Plato and fully formulated by Aristotle: clear generic distinction, a hierarchy of logical systems with the rigor of "science" and dialectic dominating the looser probabilities of rhet-oric and poetic, a tight control over the kinds of responses expected (Plato's *psychogogia,* Aristotle's *pathos*), and a visual metaphor of the relationship between the subject who speaks and object of discourse. Thus, the reaction of the philosophers to the sophists subverts the formers' attempt to separate style from substance. The sophistic style, anticipating in a fashion *écriture féminine,* runs deeper than surface "technique." To turn Buffon on his head, style *is* the woman.

But sophistic style does not exist outside of reason, in a polar opposition to it. It does not come from a kind of prior state of innocence before the formulation of logic or genre, nor does Cixous's *écriture féminine* seek a return to some pre-logical state. Both are encompassing and mixed discourses, fully in charge of the power of patriarchal logic, calling it into play on occasion. Gorgias, for exam-ple, playfully exploits causal logic in his *Encomium of Helen* as a frame for speculating on the power of speech and overturning the conventional condemnation of Helen. The "Protagoras" of Plato's dialogue self-consciously combines narrative and argument in answer to Socrates's question, Can virtue be taught?

Clement and Cixous discuss/argue the question of gender and discourse forms in the Exchange at the end of *The Newly Born Woman*. Clement argues that a "discourse of mastery," i.e., a conventional philosophical discourse, is convenient at this time for transmitting knowledge. While I agree with Clement that women need to be heard at this time speaking with the voice of philosophic authority, I resist her insistence on that discourse as the only vehicle of "democratic transmission" (138). Cixous counters with the point that "far from transmitting knowledge, [mastery] makes it [i.e., knowledge] still more inaccessible . . . [It becomes] sacred, . . . Law's dirty trick. Only those people who already have a relationship of mastery . . . who are saturated with culture, have ever dared have access to the discourse that the master gives" (139). Clement denies that a discourse other than a conventional propositional one has any power to communicate at all: communication is blocked at the boundary of "coherence." But who is given the power to define the term "coherence"? When she describes the threat to patriarchal logic in terms of mental illness, one thinks of Foucault's warning in *Madness and Civilization* that conditions like madness are culturally determined by ruling groups and precisely through discourse. Clement is suspicious of a discourse "whose coherence is literally neurotic and which has no other way to defend itself. It is not knowledge that is being conveyed there but something on the order of the poetic. . . . When it is a question of knowledge, I am talking about a body of coherent statements that is not a neurotic coherence, hence one that isn't held together by the *singular* phantasmic specialty of the one who does the conveying" (144, emphasis in original). We seem to be stuck once again in a binary opposition with women's writing, or sophistic style, as the "other" to a logic of mastery. While Clement at times acknowledges the historical formation of any discourse, at other moments she seems to deny history and any possibility of reformulation: "I see no way to conceive of a cultural system in which there would be no transmission of knowledge in the form of a coherent statement"; "the power to change ... knowledge comes through mediations that are too complex for us to judge what they might be"; "when one made use of this discourse for transmitting, it didn't matter whether one was a man or a woman" (141, 145, 146). Clement refuses to envision an alternative to a strictly logical discourse and thus insists on the irrelevance of gender to its use.

Sophistic *Nomos*

I think the sophists provide an alternative to this seemingly fixed *logos* and, by extension, to a discourse of difference through their attention to *nomos*. As we saw in the previous chapter, *nomos* refers to provisional codes (habits or customs) of social and political behavior, socially constructed and historically (even geographically) specific. The codification of any set of *nomoi* is the work of rhetoric in its constructive role; the "reading" of *nomos* in any text is rhetoric's analytic or critical function. In opposition to *logos* as a permanent and "natural" structure of law, rationality or language, *nomos* can be called into play as an alternative, designating the human, and thus necessarily discursive, construction of changeable codes. The term operates at the nexus of language and history: it signifies the relativization of *logos*—the real conditions (*nomoi*) under which texts are produced in specific times and places. Though normally applied to law, by implication the term could be taken to deny the possibility of any discourse—"literary" or "philosophic," for example—isolated from the operation of social customs and political power.

The works of the sophists themselves can be read through *nomos*. Both Gorgias and Protagoras demonstrated a sophisticated awareness of logical sequences in their use of language. But instead of moving in the direction of fixing a law of logic, their works seem designed rather to call attention to the ways patterns of reasoning came to be accepted.[10] They employed narratives to radically reconstruct their own histories in terms which opened space for difference. In Gorgias's imaginative reconstruction of Helen's abduction, desire, will, and language throw open the traditional causal logic of her case and, in so doing, dislodge a mythic source for misogynism. In Protagoras's revisionary retelling of the Promethean creation myth, we find laid out the process of the social construction of identity: an explanation of how family and school teach codes which determine the modes of expression available. Indeed, the reader is armed with that knowledge just as Prometheus armed humans with fire and the *techne* (craft, skill) to use it. Further, Protagoras has rewritten the myth he inherited from Hesiod, omitting the punishment of man by receiving woman—thoughtless Pandora, who released all the evils into the world.[11] In sum, the achievement of the sophists for contemporary readers is not "merely" a stylistic difference. A sophistic reading of sophistic style calls into question the Platonic *logos* as the intuited source and permanent structure of any discourse of knowledge and undermines *logoi* defined as "law" in the narrow sense based on divinely sanctioned, aristocratic privilege.

Nomos offers a mode of reading centered on narratives encoded in the text and in the times. Such an analytic provides a useful alternative to the attempt to discover marginalized voices marked by characteristic stylistic features. Mary Jacobus observes that, because the feminine is so effectively suppressed in Western discourse, these features cannot be counted on to appear at a surface level in texts, even by women. Displaced woman is "either unrecorded in accessible ways, or recorded in terms of man" (Jacobus 185). This same exclusion applies to what might be called a sophistic voice in the history of rhetoric. The focus on *nomos* highlights the project of rewriting histories: a project central to both to *écriture féminine* and to the sophists. Cixous seeks a writing which will "allow [a woman] to put the breaks and indispensable changes into effect in her history" (97). In the autobiographical segment of "Sorties," she describes the beginning of feminist consciousness in terms of history: "I look for myself throughout the centuries and don't see myself anywhere" (Cixous 75). Her agenda becomes rewriting history: "Phallocentrism. History has never produced or recorded anything else . . . And it is time to change. To invent the other history" (Cixous 83). Her particular historical revision in *Newly Born Woman* rereads Kleist's version of the Homeric epic to distinguish man's law from woman's law for Achilles and Penthesilea. Indeed, a number of feminist scholars are engaged in a similar process of reexamining the codes—both linguistic and "legal"—shaping women's stories. These strike me as projects of a specifically sophistic/rhetorical nature.

Feminist Sophistics: Revising Logic Through Narrative

Here we return to Spivak's reformulation of a historical question for feminists: "What is man that the itinerary of his desire creates [the] text" of Western phallogocentrism? ("Displacement" 186). Both Spivak and Cixous consider the question from the different perspectives of father and mother at the moment of birth. From that moment, Freud claims that a different logic is in play for the female, "since maternity is proved by the senses whereas paternity is a surmise based on a deduction and a premiss" (*Moses and Monotheism* 153, quoted in Cixous 100). When this logic of deduction—the assignment of the name of the father to the son—becomes the privileged source of meaning and reference, as it clearly does for Freud, a challenge to privilege seeks a different logic, beginning from a different desire, tracing a new "itinerary." The point is not to fix irremediably two essential lines of logic, man's and woman's, but to locate legally and historically the falsely naturalized logic of patriarchy (as emerging from a particular set of *nomoi*) in contrast to an alternative experienced historically by women and creating necessarily different discursive products.[12] In reading texts from the "discourse of man," Spivak recommends that women as literary critics superimpose a "suitable allegory" in order to break into received readings. The force of resistance in such "misreadings" should, of course, be "made scrupulously explicit" (Spivak, "Displacement" 186).

Mary Jacobus articulates another alternative to the "quest for specificity" (38)—i.e., for particular stylistic features—in the "drift toward narrative in recent works of feminist criticism" (41). It pleases the feminist critic, she says, to "light on a text whose story is the same as hers" (41). Jacobus's own reading of Maggie Tulliver from George Eliot's *Mill on the Floss* re-evaluates Maggie's story, saving it from the condemnation of the "men of maxims," in whose eyes Maggie's behavior is so illogical, her actions so implausible. Jacobus reads into

Eliot's Maggie the collusion of "error" as a masculine concept with traditional, "factual" history: "Error must creep in where there's a story to tell, especially a woman's story. . . . Maggie's 'wrong-doing and absurdity' . . . not only puts her on the side of error in the discourse of man [which in the story is voiced by her brother Tom] but gives her a history" (48). In denying the "logic" of true and good behavior status as a universal and permanent *logos* and redefining it as a hegemonic code or *nomoi,* Jacobus relocates value and virtue in Maggie's world. The feminist reader recaptures a character "engulfed by masculine logic and language" and ending in a "swirl of (im)possibility" (51). Ultimately, meaning for Maggie emerges directly out of her experience of being deprived of a formal education—an outcome of the masculine code under which her story plays out. Rhetoric as the art of the possible is obligated neither to the "factual" nor even to the probabilities Aristotle demands for poetry. As Nietzsche explained, rhetoric, like history, is always on the side of "error" in the non-moral sense, over Truth in a metaphysical scheme ("Truth and Lies"). It always reads the "real," both present and past, in terms of future possibilities, specifying "real" for whom, under what conditions, and toward what ends. These are the questions reopened by Jacobus for Maggie after her sentencing by male judges.

In a third case, Nancy K. Miller provides examples of feminist readings which take a revision of logic through narrative as their central strategy. In "Arachnologies: The Woman, The Text, and the Critic," she retells Ovid's story of Arachne to demonstrate a kind of reading "against the weave of indifferentiation" (272). While often remembered by a cruel metaphor only as the spider who spins a meaningless web, victim of Athena's vanity, Arachne is reinstated in Miller's account in the process of weaving a beautiful tapestry with its own story of women raped and destroyed by Zeus. Miller calls her own technique "overreading" an "underread" text. The goal of overreading is not only to retrieve a text from an anonymity it may have been forced into by a philosophical or "masculine" discourse; it seeks to recover a fuller narrative, to identify the social conditions of its production (N. Miller 287). Miller, like the sophists, works against teleology to open possibilities for reinterpretation.

In another essay, "Emphasis Added: Plots and Plausibilities in Women's Fiction," Miller expresses most directly the political signifi-cance of narrative: "The power and pleasure of the weak come from circumventing the laws of contingency and circulation" (42). Mean-ing and legitimacy derive not from a universal sense of coherence or logic, but through a kind of rhetorical hermeneutics, from the "*doxa* of socialities"; "plausibility then is an effect of reading through a grid of concordance" (N. Miller 36). "Concordance" is another word for the socially constructed, and thus gender specific, patterns of customs the Greeks codified as *nomoi*. Miller calls her practice of reading for those patterns *italicization:* a method of rereading "feminine" fiction devalued by the "male" grid of concordance. This is a form of empha-sis which credits "the extravagant wish for a story that would turn out differently" (N. Miller 44). Miller denies that "fictions of desire behind the desiderata of fiction" are universal constructs; they are organizations of the dominant culture. In so doing, Miller addresses a problem I find with current work in narrative which may seem related to the role I assign to rhetoric in this speculation. The claim of universality for narrative logics, whose formulae are generally reducible to an Aristotelian syntax, fails to allow for difference (e.g., Fisher). Under such paradigms, the men of maxims will still be deciding whose stories are "coherent and faithful." The same problem occurs in analyses of rhetorical *topoi* that take those "places" for argument as ontological categories (D'Angelo).

What I have discovered through this exploration is that, though the sophists may not be "feminists," current feminists are becoming sophists in the best sense of the word by describing rhetorical solu-tions to the crucial problem of defining a theory with the most power for changing women's lives. Sophistic rhetoric enables a feminist reading/writing practice of breaking into the "received histories" of the discourse of man (Spivak, "Displacement" 186). Rewriting/rereading texts in terms of the narrative logic of difference opens avenues not only in literature but also in the history of rhetoric. Narratizing the social-historical differential specifically in rhetoric will trace the diversion of women's discursive energy into the school room and drawing room, allowing a redefined "rhetoric" to include letters, texts on manners and education, and perhaps other forms as yet unidentified (see Bizzell and Herzberg). It allows not only for the identification of new works but also offers a way to reread hegemonic texts as well, tracing the itinerary of male desire with a new critical perspective. Showing how feminist theory and literary critical work enacts practices adumbrated by the democratic rhetoric of the sophists provides a way to recover a range of marginal voices in the history of rhetoric. Reciprocally, outlining the connections with sophistic rhetoric in current feminist reading and writing may offer increased leverage for dislodging the patriarchal institutions whose foundations were laid during the sophists' time.

4

Our ordinary citizens, though occupied with the pursuits of industry, are still fair judges of public matters; for, unlike any other nation, regarding him who takes no part in these duties not as unambitious but as useless, we Athenians are able to judge at all events . . . and instead of looking on discussion as a stumbling-block in the way of action, we think it an indispensable preliminary to any wise action at all.

Pericles's Funeral Oration from
Thucydides, *History of the Peloponnesian War*

SOPHISTIC PEDAGOGY,
THEN AND NOW

I T IS NO exaggeration to say that in the field of Greek education the Sophists accomplished a veritable revolution" (59). Henri Marrou's provocative assessment of the sophists' educational achievement calls to mind descriptions of changes in composition teaching we have seen and participated in since the early sixties (Connors et al.). The precise nature of both those revolutions, however, and what sorts of connections we can draw between them, are in dispute. Urgent questions for the field of rhetoric and composition today concern relationships between the history of rhetoric and contemporary pedagogy and between the state and the school. On the extremes of the history/composition axis, there are, on the one hand, a desire to liberate the teaching of writing today from the history of rhetoric (Knoblauch and Brannon) and, on the other, a drive to reinstate parts of that history relatively wholesale (Corbett). In the middle, scholars work toward revising or adapting historical materials for today's context (Lunsford & Ede, D'Angelo, Welch). The politics/ composition problematic engages a passionate segment of the profession, many of whom question the role of the writing course in a capitalist economy which distributes its goods unevenly among classes, races, and genders (Bizzell, "Beyond"; Ohmann; Berlin, "Ideology"; Bartholomae). My aim in this chapter is to examine the sophists' educational praxis within the direct democracy of Athens as a way of reflecting on the political possibilities for composition teaching today. My assumption that there is a legitimate way to use the history of rhetoric to inform current work in the teaching of writing will not lead to a recommendation that teachers import sophistic teaching techniques wholesale into the classrooms of late-twentieth-century American universities. Instead, I want to argue that analyzing the relationships among the first sophists' social theory, their pedagogy, and the functioning of the democracy in their time can help us evaluate the political dimensions of composition pedagogies in our own. In this final chapter, I will examine several readings of the sophists' contributions as educators, interweaving references to the contemporary scene of composition teaching, in order to suggest how the sophists can indicate progressive directions for composition teachers today.

The Sophists as Educators

At the most basic level, the sophists' contribution could be seen as marking historically the "invention" of teaching itself as a profession. Marrou asserts that the sophists were "above all teachers" (49). Discounting arguments that they could be characterized by any unified "philosophy," he casts his praise for the education they offered in terms of its cultural standing as a profession:

> They deserve our respect as the great forerunners, as the first teachers
> of advanced education, appearing at a time when Greece had known
> nothing but sports-trainers, foremen, and, in the academic field,
> humble school-masters. In spite of the sarcasm thrown at them by
> the Socratics with their conservative prejudices, I shall continue to
> respect them because, primarily, they were professional men for
> whom teaching was an occupation whose commerical success bore
> witness to its intrinsic value and its social utility. (49)

In centuries prior to the fifth, a young man from the aristocratic class would have been "adopted" in an informal way and trained in performance of fitting "words and deeds" by an older male friend of the family, a relationship for which Phoenix's commitment to Achilles is the best-documented model (*Iliad* IX). But in the middle of the fifth century, a small number of exceptionally qualified travelling intellectuals began to gather young men able to pay a fee into small "colloquia" or seminar groups for three or four years of political education.[1] Though Kennedy warns that "exactly what went on in the schools of the sophists is not well known" (*Rhetoric* 25), we have a number of details about sophistic education which together offer a picture of a comprehensive instruction in language use over a wide range of subjects but concentrating on political science. As teachers, the sophists used a variety of discourse forms. Their long set speeches were delivered in public performances or in smaller gatherings in the homes of wealthy citizens. Students would probably copy, memorize, and recite the speeches themselves, as well as using them for models in preparing speeches of their own on set topics or public issues. Another important method in sophistic education employed question and answer; indeed, Protagoras is said by Diogenes Laertius to have invented the "Socratic" method (Kerferd 33). He taught his pupils to praise and censure the same case, probably using a textbook he had written called *Contrary Arguments* (Guthrie, *Sophists* 181–82). The text probably contained sets of contradictory statements—commonplaces—which the student would memorize and employ in constructing legal cases and arguments for the assembly.

The structure of sophistic education reflected in smaller scale the form of the democratic society it served. It differed from the older aristocratic practice, wherein a young man would learn through close association (sometimes including sexual intimacy) with a single older man of the same class, and also from the ascetic philosophic schools of the Pythagoreans. The young man, who had already finished a primary education, would benefit from the excitement and stimulation of living and perhaps traveling with a charismatic intellectual leader and a group of his fellows engaged in the same studies (Kerferd 30). Though some historians, following Plato, envision sophistic teaching as a matter of entrancing or impressing students with expertise—Marrou speaks of stage-effects and infatuation (50)—we could compare situations such as the dawn meeting at Callias's house represented in *Protagoras* with the excitement of a late-night discussion after the talk of a visiting lecturer, and the extended experience of sophistic education with the intensity of a committed writing or reading group or an advanced summer seminar. Missing from our contemporary picture, however, is a primary feature of Athenian education in the fifth century: the prospect of taking the knowledge and skill mastered in the class directly into practice in the running of the polis. The modern parallel would have the student graduating from these intense group sessions into a seat in the legislature or into a job as a litigating attorney or labor organizer. In fact, many students enter and leave universities in the United States with little sense of their location in or responsibility to a public sphere (Spivak, *Worlds* 98–100). The desire to change that situation sends us with some urgency to an era when the connection between classroom and society was much closer.

Plato's scorn for the sophists' practice of receiving pay for teaching draws attention to their new status as professional educators.[2] The philosopher helps us to mark a historical moment when the teaching of language performance skill and cultural wisdom passed from the public poet and older family friends among the elite to a professional class. Though the complaint may seem like an ethical nicety today, there was some moral taint attached to selling one's labor in classical Greece (Ober 135–56). But a more probable explanation for the Platonic objection sees it as an aristocratic resistance to making available the skills of governance to anyone, regardless of birth, who could pay for them. In sixth-century Athens the shift from birth to wealth as a criterion of rule was a major step on the way to democracy. One of Solon's major reforms was to open up membership in the ruling elite, i.e., the opportunity to serve as *archon,* to any Athenian who fell within the top one or two categories of wealth according to the census (Ober 60–63). The effect of the change, as of the sophists' instruction for pay in the next century, was increased political mobility. So, to expand Marrou's statement, we can appreciate the sophists as professional teachers when we see that the evolution of that very category signaled major political and social change attendant on the democracy.

The twentieth-century "revolution" in the teaching of composition was born out of a period with similar goals. The civil rights and women's movements of the sixties and early seventies provided some avenues for social mobility, while large-scale public protests of the

Vietnam war and on issues of ecology and nuclear energy provided
the vehicle for a wider participation in state affairs in the United
States than any time since the labor movements of the thirties. While
there was certainly much dynamic rhetorical behavior going on outside the classroom during this period, the teaching of composition
was also involved as new student-centered pedagogies fueled resistance to university establishments unresponsive to student needs.
Works from the expressive school in the sixties and seventies advanced
the democratic goal of giving students a voice (Berlin, *Reality* 150–
53).[3] Open admissions policies, won through protests for equal opportunity in education, drew attention to the centrality of literacy for
social change and the role of the composition class in teaching that
skill. Mina Shaughnessy's work is the best-known contribution to
the democratic enfranchisement of lower class students through the
academy. Her analysis of the errors of basic writers changed teachers'
perceptions of such students and offered a method by which to
teach standard English as an alternative to non-standard dialects her
students brought to the classroom. Despite the derailment of the
protest movements of the sixties, a mission for the composition
course as a site for re-democritization—not only as a vehicle for social
mobility, but for re-enfranchisement in a political climate marked by
apathy and distance—has been sustained in the field of composition
and rhetoric into the late eighties.[4] Though historians have charted
the reversals of liberatory gains through the recession of the seventies
and the roll-backs of the eighties (Shor, *Culture Wars;* Aronowitz
and Giroux), many compositionists continue to explore the role of
the writing classroom in empowering students as participants in the
democracy. I find the historical precedent for this approach to literacy
instruction in the educational theory and practice of the first sophists,
and it is to their politically motivated education for democracy I will
ultimately return. But first, however, I will take up two issues that
arise in discussions both of the sophists and of contemporary composition pedagogy that pose problems for democratic education. They
are questions about the status of the individual and about the ethical
implications of a technical education.

Education of the Individual Intellect

A historical focus on the development of democracy notes the growth of *homonoia*, like-mindedness, among the citizens of the polis. But a competing theme in fifth-century Greek cultural development is the awareness of individual consciousness (see chapter 2). One problem for the classical historian is how to reach an understanding of the balance between individual and group. As Werner Jaeger puts it, "Only at this stage [in history] . . . are such problems as those of freedom and authority, or education for citizenship and education for leadership, conceived and answered" (288). This problem emerges very sharply with the sophists—theorists, educators, and even architects of democracy but at the same time charismatic aliens, each with a distinctive personality, individual teachers of small groups of economically privileged students. Jaeger, pre-eminent commentator on Greek education, casts the shift in pedagogical practice from the old aristocracy to the new democracy in terms of the solution to a political problem: on what basis would an education for the new citizenry of the *polis* be established other than the inheritance of excellence through noble blood? He answers it in terms of the individual. The intellectual capacities of individuals in the political community will serve as the new determinant of power and authority (287). And it is the sophists who will create and implement the education for this new intellectual elite: "The aim of the education movement led by the sophists was not to educate the people, but to educate the leaders of the people" (290). Jaeger sees the sophistic movement as an embodiment of the new rationalism; its central educational task is developing "consciousness." This focus subordinates the political— the democratic group experience—to the personal: "The rationalization of political education was only a special case of the rationalization of all life within Athens; for now more than ever before the end of life was achievement, success" (291–92). Comparing the classical period of Greece with the Renaissance, Jaeger weighs the individual heavily against the community: "An entirely new and fundamentally individualist type of culture was coming into being—for the sophists were individualists, however much they might talk of education to serve the community and training in the arete of a good citizen" (297).

Of course, Jaeger's larger project, *Paideia,* concerns the equation of teaching with general culture, a concept he gives the sophists credit for creating (313). Acknowledging the interconnection between culture and state in classical Athens, he describes the goal of education as creating for the student an experience of shared culture founded on membership in political community (287). For the sophists, the state is the focus and source of educational energy (321). Jaeger gives the sophists credit for making the Greeks conscious of culture (303) in a society in which the only universal culture resided in the state (300). Thus he emphasizes the significance of democratic political theory in understanding the role of education in the Athenian democracy.

But because Jaeger focuses on only a small number of highly qualified rhetors and ignores the issue of communication with a larger mass of citizens (Ober 13), consciousness becomes an exclusive property. This interpretive screen leads him to an elitist view of the sophists: they offer education for the few, but based on mental capacity rather than aristocratic birth. Jaeger sanctions that form of hierarchy through his reversion to Plato's argument for in-born excellence, asserting that "the chief qualities of a statesman cannot be acquired" (290). The sophistic project becomes validated by reading it in terms of inner development of the individual. This solution distorts the sophists' educational practice to fit a Platonic mold; their goal is described as a shaping of the soul (314), a concept to which no sophist would lay claim. Jaeger is able to do this because he rejects a reading of Greek democracy based on anthropological theory, focusing instead on leadership based on natural ability. Minimizing the achievement of political rule through communal discourse, Jaeger sees the sophistic education falling apart on the ethical issue of individual rights in conflict with the state. Jaeger acknowledges, as do Ober and others, that in classical Athens individual freedom was subordinate to group interests; there was no concept of "inalienable rights" in the sense that modern liberalism has defined them (Ober 10; Holmes 118; J. Finley 154–55). The individual's relation to the democracy is instead envisioned in terms of a striving for power against the interests of the whole community (321). Taking Callicles from Plato's *Gorgias* and Thrasymachus from the *Republic* as examples of the powerful individual suppressed by the mediocrity of the democratic mass, Jaeger finds an ethical vacuum in sophistic education inadequate to resolve this problem. He sees the political ethics of Protagoras foundering on the new individualism which allowed the natural leader to question the laws of the state. The sophists seem to fall between two ethical eras—the older Greece guided by traditional practices and gods, and the new metaphysics of Plato's fourth-century philosophy.

In pointing out the contradiction for modern societies between a Christian morality based on the individual (evolving out of the Platonic concept of the soul) and a communal politics inherited from Greece, Jaeger identifies a very modern problem in American schooling and public life. A powerful ideology of individualism works against a sense of community both in the classroom and outside. I will ultimately argue that sophistic teaching offers resources for bridging that gap. But Jaeger's description of the sophists builds the priority of the individual into sophistic educational theory by fragmenting the theory into three parts: formal, factual, and political/ethical. The first two derive from different ways of viewing the mind: as a receptacle for objects (or even perceptions of objects) or as an organ with its own internal structure. The third he attributes to Protagoras alone, providing a positive picture of sophistic education as a mediation between individual and group:

> It differed from both the formal and the encyclopaedic methods by treating man not abstractly, as a lone individual, but as a member of the community; and thereby it gave him a firm position in the world of values, and made intellectual culture one part of the great whole which was human arete. This method also was intellectual education; however, it treated the mind neither formally nor factually, but as conditioned by the social order. (293)

But what Jaeger gives the sophists in one breath, he takes away with another. Despite his apparent approval of the social construction of ethics and intellect in Protagorean education, he finds that such training failed to "attack the deeper problems of morality and the state" (293), problems soluble only through the philosophical political theories of Plato and Aristotle. While Jaeger provides a valuable historical perspective on a modern problem, his fragmentation of sophistic pedagogy reinscribes that dilemma. The sophists remain trapped in a conflict between individual and state rather than offering us a way to reconceive the relationship between cognitive development and group action.

The priority of mental activity over group communication in Jaeger's view of the sophists resembles the way writing is conceived by cognitive psychologists investigating the writing process today. Researchers like Flower and Hayes build a model as an analog of the mental processes of the writer; they take the single individual as the subject of inquiry. Further, they suggest pedagogical applications based on their work. Called "formalists" by Stephen North, they posit a model of mental activity during writing as a way of seeking understanding of what actually happens when writers write (242–45). Though social factors enter into their models at points, their focus is on the individual. Bizzell's now canonical critique of their work is based on this observation ("Cognition"). She contrasts their agenda with that of sociolinguists and others engaged in "outer-directed research" more concerned with the interchange between individual and community resulting in discourse. If rhetoric through history helps us to understand and make decisions about composition teaching today, then relying too heavily on views of the sophists that minimize their contribution to democratic discourse theory and practice could have the effect of supporting a general approach to writing instruction today which, in tune with a society immersed in an ideology of individualism, looks too narrowly at the single writer as a site of language production. In terms of Jaeger's fragmentation of sophistic teaching theory, this emphasis would keep a formal investigation of the mind separate from a political/ethical inquiry into the relation between discourse, political action, and social responsibility.

Kennedy's classification of the sophists also emphasizes their individualism, but not as the locus of cognitive development. He lumps together the older sophists with Isocrates and the Second Sophists of second-century A.D. Rome under the heading "Sophistic Rhetoric" (chapter 3), by which he means "the older tradition of imitating a successful orator, with little or no conscious conceptualization of the techniques involved" (*Rhetoric* 25). This typology emphasizes personal influence and rote learning rather than technique and looks to the teacher as a model, a superior individual whom the students emulate. Kennedy's classification is compatible with Jaeger's description of the sophists as advocates of a pedagogy of personal advancement for a few students possessing superior ability. Indeed, both positions rest on natural ability. Again, a number of contemporary composition texts reenact in certain ways both the method and the philosophy of Kennedy's view of the sophists as educators of the individual intellect. Students under some expressivist pedagogies model the process of a successful, charismatic individual such as Donald Murray or Peter Elbow. Murray's spontaneous public writings recall stories of Gorgias and Hippias, who were said to be able to compose extemporaneously on any topic. The attraction to a charismatic figure includes Socrates, a model for Elbow, with the sophists.[5] Of course, these teachers differ from Kennedy's sophists in their "conscious conceptualization" of techniques such as free-writing; indeed, this demystification of writing technique has been one of their primary contributions to writing pedagogy. It would not be fair to insist that their methods rely most heavily on the author's natural abilities. Both Murray and Elbow assert the importance of practice, advising the production of multiple drafts. In fact, the whole process movement—with its strong emphasis on producing a quantity of text—could be said to have shifted emphasis from a "vitalist" notion of writing emerging mysteriously from talented writers after their exposure to prose models to a "practice" and "technique" oriented pedagogy. But, paradoxically, these teachers are engaged at the same time in a remystification through such advice as "listen to the voice of the text" (Murray) and accounts of "cooking" (Elbow). Such advice fits with the focus on the individual in expressivist pedagogy. But an expressivist pedagogy that remains unaware of the political implications of such advice is a problem for a democratic education. In some cases, awareness is not the problem. Elbow explicitly rejects the liberatory political pedagogy of Paulo Freire. He advises writing teachers in North American universities to refrain from "bamboozling" students by announcing, " 'We are not trying to change the world here' " and " 'This is not education designed to make you free. . . . I cannot here help you liberate yourself'" (94).

Behind the limitations of Kennedy's and Jaeger's interpretations of sophistic education and the contemporary pedagogies with which I have associated them stands the question of the subject. As inheritors of eighteenth-century classical liberalism, many of us will read this socialization process with a strong sense of the importance of the "negative rights" of the citizen not to be interfered with by the state, rights guaranteed by the social compact (Holmes). We believe ourselves to be imbued with the "inalienable right" to be ignored by the state. Expressive compositionists' work serves a liberal self with inalienable rights of non-interference. In this pedagogy, success is anticipated to the degree the writer can free him- or herself from the constraints of the crowd and "be himself" (Berlin, *Reality* 154).[6] In democratic Greece, however, though there was a division between public and private spheres (*ta koina* and *ta idia*), duties outweighed individual "rights" (Holmes 118). Thucydides's Pericles announced that people unwilling to conceive of themselves in political terms were useless to the *polis* (II, 1.40).[7]

The "subject" of sophistic education according to Protagoras is a social subject—"straightened" by indoctrination in the ways of the polis through home and school measures and responsible to the community to develop a sense of civic virtue. But Gorgias, on the other hand, in the *Helen* shows us a different kind of subject—the individual receiving language and acting on it (Segal 104–110). Gorgias's speculation on the power of logos explores the pleasure and force of language, but also places internal experience—e.g., Helen's seduction by Paris—in a context of specific historical and social conditions, reflecting on the effects on others of choices made under the influence of logos. The *Palamedes* likewise alludes to social obligation in a defense of the person who revealed Odysseus's attempt to avoid public service. Though these two versions of the subject of sophistic pedagogy—Protagoras's and Gorgias's—seem to reflect the ideological opposition in composition pedagogy today between a social as against a liberal/individualistic approach, I would propose that a mediation of that conflict might be sought in a version of the sophists combining the insights of the two major sophists as they imply a subject. An integrated picture of the subject of sophistic pedagogy defines the individual both as the location of a separate mind perceiving distinctive visual and aural stimuli and as member of a group of like-minded individuals with responsibility to participate in the democracy. In the current field of rhetoric and composition, the attempt to forge a similar integration appears in such forms as the research orientation now called "social cognition" and in the development of collaborative writing and editing in composition classrooms (see Trimbur). The phenomenon of differentiation of social groups in modern society complicates a simple opposition between individual and social subjectivities and leads to the possibility for multiple and competing "subject positions" among students (Laclau and Mouffe). While the complexity of social organization in twentieth-century first-world nations is not anticipated by the sophists, their texts do provide openings into the issue of social difference. Gorgias's choice of the predicament of a woman under sexual pressure invites thought about gender difference; "Protagoras's" reference to his vulnerable status as a foreigner in Athens forces a recognition of ethnic or "national" difference. More than these specific contents, the sophists offer discursive strategies that can be employed to identify and negotiate differences among social groups. Such strategies—their nature and use—come under examination as *techne,* providing another historical pigeon-hole into which the sophists are sometimes placed. Like the view of sophists as educators of the individual intellect, this classification also requires careful examination.

Technical Education: Practice and Ethics

While Jaeger asserted that the Protagorian myth specifically subordinated technical knowledge to cultural understanding, thus making possible culture as opposed to "civilization" (300), Marrou finds that "the revolution in education that has come to be known as Sophistry seems to have had a technical rather than a political origin" (48).[8] A similar interpretation of writing instruction today classifies it as an instrumental skill. This interpretation of sophistic education has a prestigious precedent in Plato's *Phaedrus,* where Socrates denigrates the sophists as the heirs of Sicilian handbook writers (¶266–269). He defines their contribution exclusively in terms of its introduction of formal devices of invention, organization, and style used for composing speeches.[9] While Phaedrus offers the contents of the handbooks to comprise a definition of "rhetoric," Socrates informs him that these rules and forms are merely the "niceties," only "preliminaries" of the art. There follows a catalog of rules about arrangement, arguments from probability, dicta concerning speech length, figures of speech, and parts of speech in which all the sophists are mentioned by name.

This technical emphasis denies or ignores a connection between the sophists' teaching and their theories of social order, language, and perception; it disallows a "philosophic" base for their project (Kennedy, *Rhetoric* 18–22). Plato is, of course, working here toward a redefinition of rhetoric—a rhetoric built on dialectic, grounded in metaphysics, and thus a "true" rhetoric. The rhetoric he disdains is only a "knack" (*Gorgias*)—a set of techniques or practices wielded handily by the teacher/rhetor and taught to others but without a foundation in truth or a responsibility for their content or outcome beyond an short-term utility. Two forms of this reductive definition with implications for contemporary composition teaching are the relation of practice to theory and the problem of ethics in a skills course.

Practice

According to Marrou, Protagoras's political teaching had "a purely practical aim" (50). Though Marrou defends the sophists as humanists, by which he means generalists (57), he sees their contribution as practical and thus superficial. Despite the fact that they set in

motion a number of ideas, says Marrou, "their fundamental utilitari-
anism would . . . have prevented them from penetrating [any one of
them] to the depths" (57). The assumption here is that practice is
divorced from theory or philosophy—out of touch with deeper understanding.

This dichotomy has been a prominent feature of the composition
discipline over the last decades. There has been on the one hand the
desire to recognize and acknowledge the hard work of composition
teachers who spend many hours in the classroom and do not do
"research." Establishing "composition" as a legitimate university field
has entailed a heated defense of teachers as noble practitioners—
front-line soldiers in a battle for literacy—as against ivory-tower
literature scholars for whom teaching is secondary to theoretical or
philosophic activities: i.e., scholarly research. In Stephen North's *The
Making of Knowledge in Composition,* "practitioners," though they are
granted a knowledge-making role, are kept separate from "philosophers" and other theoretical types. North keeps in place the division,
simply overturning the Platonic critique of teaching practice. He
claims that practitioners "make knowledge," but it is of a different
type from philosophic knowledge and should not claim its form or
status. His gesture, however, has the effect of reinforcing the division
between practice and theory. On the other hand, there is a move to
fuse the roles of compositionists as teachers and theorists/researchers
(Berthoff; Phelps, *Composition;* Harkin).

A deep understanding of the sophists as teachers whose practice
constitutes a "theory" can give composition teachers a historical perspective from which to reconsider that relationship. Alternative definitions of "practice" offer ways to revalue sophistic teaching as a
profession clearly distinguished from the detachment of philosophy
in its engagement in social action. This understanding is achieved
through an association of "practice" with philosophical pragmatism.
Cornell West explains philosophical pragmatism out of American
John Dewey as antirealist in ontology, antifoundationalist in epistemology, and detranscendentalist in terms of the subject (Stephanson).[10] The focus on action in pragmatism helps us to understand
the sophists' concentration on teaching within the larger context

of a particular social vision rather than as merely opportunistic or utilitarian in a reductive sense. In this light, Plato's attempt to diminish the sophists' practice merely to a technical process can be seen not only as his distortion of their project through a philosophic lens that divides theory from practice, but also as an effort to invalidate a specifically democratic political content in their educational program. In the contemporary scene, validation of practice in this philosophical sense would go beyond the idea of "teacher as researcher"—the use of the classroom to collect data for experiments. Rather, it redefines the classroom as a collective inquiry into the function of discourse in a democracy, in which students and teacher are equally engaged. From a somewhat older tradition, the Marxist-based pedagogy of Paulo Freire emphasizes the necessity of education as praxis, a form of action informed by reflection (Freire 100). The sophists' "practice," not confined to the classroom, made them into the pre-eminent public intellectuals of their era—a role that should, I believe, be sought by composition teachers today. While this role will be discussed more fully below, I wish to turn first to the pressing question of ethics which always arises in discussions of practice and technique.

Ethics

Another problem with describing the sophists solely in terms of their technical innovations raises a question about the ethical force of teaching mere forms without care for the "content" that fills them. Again we see the effect of the Platonic opposition of rhetoric to philosophy. According to Plato, because the strategies of the sophists only provide ways of manipulating *doxa* without leading, as does Platonic dialectic, to Truth, and because Truth is synonymous with Good, rhetorical techniques of the sophists carry no guarantee of ethical rectitude. This issue is handled most directly in *Gorgias,* wherein Socrates asks if Gorgias will be responsible for the student who misuses his teaching. The "Gorgias" in the dialogue denies that he teaches ethics. Though other portions of the Gorgian fragments support that stance, some commentators disagree that Gorgias could have held such a position (Barrett 15). But it is more important to reestablish a sophistic rather than a Platonic frame for the question than just to leave the issue as a matter of specific historical data about individual figures. The problem of ethics in the sophists overall is related to their epistemology; i.e., to their insistence on the relativity of meaning and, consequently, value. According to Gorgias's treatise *On the Nonexistent* and in Protagoras's "human as measure" doctrine, questions of value must be referred to subjective perception and to the historical and geographical specificity of local custom. Ethics, in other words, are inseparable from *ethe,* a word meaning "haunts," or, even more colloquially, "hang outs" and by extension "habits" or "practices." Throughout the *Protagoras,* for example, the elder sophist continually positioned his discourse about ideological indoctrination in education locally, using such formulations as "And the Athenians, especially, your fellow citizens no less than other men . . ." and "Your countrymen are right to . . ." (¶324c).[11] Though there is no philosophic "good" grounding the sophistic project, questions of ethics permeate their work. Through reference to the formation of ethical norms within communities, the sophists go beyond total relativism—a hedonistic self-interest—to a discourse about enlightened self-interest based in the notion of "self" as constituted by the community.

In the contemporary context, those composition programs concentrating solely on "techniques" such as process, free-writing, and sentence-combining, and which remain unreflective about the ends to which "good writing" will be put, open themselves to the classical ethical critique of the sophists: that they provide a skill in an unspecified ethical context. To translate this evaluation into the modern university curriculum, these "sophists" would be like those who teach style, advertising, political debate, or business writing—any kind of facility with the dominant discourse—without reflection built into the pedagogy on the ends toward which its students will use the skills they learn. Though it is, of course, impossible to control the uses of discourse, composition pedagogies can be judged on the basis of whether or not they introduce an ethical perspective through a critical evaluation of their aims. The sophists' own reflections on knowledge formation have been described by Jaeger as a "sociology of knowledge," a critical framework from which to evaluate the products of its processes. As sociologists of knowledge, the sophists anticipate writing-across-the-curriculum programs, which have the potential to provide critical perspective from outside disciplinary frames of reference. Another way to see the ethical question in connection with composition instruction traces it along the lines of the split of composition from its theoretical basis in literature. Without the traditional humanistic understanding of literature as the vehicle for transmitting permanent human values, compositionists who wish to define the course outside of the pure functionality of technique have turned to the history of rhetoric. This "rhetorical turn" (Bizzell, "Beyond") can be described as the current version of the sophistic counter-response to the Platonic critique. Kinneavy ("Humanities"), for example, locates composition teaching in the earliest tradition of "liberal education," found in Isocrates. Richard Lanham, who calls the ethics conundrum "The 'Q' Question" after its appearance in Quintilian, concludes that the history of rhetoric indicates ethical outcomes when motives of formal pleasure, competition, and purpose are balanced against each other. Bizzell ("Beyond") has recently argued for a more open reference to ethics in composition teaching— an ethics based on the desire to improve the material and intellectual circumstances of life for members of the community to which we belong. She advocates a pedagogy that takes seriously its mandate from the democracy enfranchising it—to provide equal opportunity for all its members and investigate injustice and inequity wherever they currently operate, hence validating an ethical imperative.

The political context for the Platonic ethical critique focuses attention on the sophistic project as the central mechanism of the democracy. For the sophists, the process of democratic decision-making did not guarantee the outcome of particular questions measured against a permanent standard, but the sophistic pedagogy should be granted the ethical force of the political process it supported. The association with democracy provides, in my view, a more compelling framework within which to describe sophistic pedagogy than either the notion of a rational education of individual consciousness or the concentration on sophists as technicians.

Education for Democracy

Sophistic teaching practice fueled a new political engine forged in the sixth and fifth centuries. The sophists redirected the emphasis in higher education, balancing instruction in aristocratic behavior and skill in arms, central to the status of the warrior/aristocrat at least from the Dark Ages to mid-fifth century, with a much greater attention spent on the new *arete* essential for democracy: the ability to create accounts of communal possibilities through persuasive speech.[12] In the case of the sophists, we see the very first education for empowerment, as their teaching-for-fees allowed anyone with the money access to power in the assembly, council, and courts.

Though they were outsiders, the sophists were all anchored in Athenian democracy. Protagoras acted as adviser to Pericles during the formative decades of the mid-fifth century. Gorgias, as a diplomat from Sicily, probably spoke before members of the Athenian council if not the assembly and also offered public speeches on political topics. He was instrumental in popularizing the epideictic speech, the origin of the public lecture and vital instrument in the formation of political thought and cultural values. Because they engaged in a range of public discourse activities including teaching, both shaping and advancing a political agenda through their talk, the sophists could be termed the first public intellectuals in a democracy. This stance is what distinguishes them from the isolated philosophical schools of the Pythagoreans and the aristocratic warrior/mentors from past eras. Though Socrates himself appears to have engaged in the same kind of small group conversations as the sophists, his notion of the philosopher as gadfly—private, solitary, and necessarily separate from the mass in the democracy—removes him from the process of decision-making. Plato, Isocrates, and Aristotle, on the other hand, all borrowed from the sophistic model of the public intellectual. Havelock notes the interrelation of politics and university education in Plato and Aristotle (*Temper* 20). But the sophists created the model and used it more closely with the democracy than any of their successors.

The "Protagoras" in Plato's dialogue provides the most complete explanation of the integration of education with the state. A student who comes to Protagoras will learn "good judgment [*euboulia*] in both private and public affairs, so as to manage the household in the best way and to act and speak the most powerfully in the city" (¶319). The implications of this definition for an education of civic "virtue" are many. The continuity between the private and public spheres, the link between speaking and acting, and the emphasis on good judgment as opposed to value-free utility are keystones of sophistic pedagogy. The sophists "directed the power of their writing and teaching toward raising people's consciousness of their attributes as social creatures and of their identity as individuals" (Barrett 36). If Protagoras's formulation does not predate the division of organized human activities into public and private spheres, especially where women are concerned (Elshtain), it does presuppose a continuity of decision-making power between those spheres, a capacity for judgment in general based on discourse. Of course, the sophists were most concerned with the civic world, most specifically the functioning of the democracy, for which the participants in sophistic education were preparing themselves. Despite differences between fifth-century Greek democracy and our own, understanding the political orientation of sophistic education is instructive for those seeking an education more responsive to contemporary political possibilities.

"Protagoras produced for the first time in human history a theoretical basis for participatory democracy" (Kerferd 144). In the process of elaborating his defense for a pedagogy of *arete*, Protagoras outlines a contemporary plan for democratic education from childhood to adulthood based on an evolutionary account of human development toward social order. Whereas we earlier examined the myth as an example of a creative form of history-writing (chapter 1) and as a feature of "orality" (chapter 2), here we see it as the foundation for democratic education. In the myth, an interpretive question arises on the exact status of *aidos* (respect) and *dike* (justice), qualities granted to humans by Zeus and necessary for organizing in social groups. While Havelock has argued for that third stage of the myth as Plato's addition because it seems to give natural status to the qualities necessary for rule, thus obviating the need for teaching, Kerferd argues that the qualities are not given in equal shares to all

and that Zeus provides in the myth for the possibility of someone
not having them at all. The significance of Kerferd's reading is that
it explains how Protagoras prepares the way for his teaching of civic
arete (142–43). Protagoras praises the Athenians for allowing anyone
(subject, of course, to the restrictions of citizenship) to participate in
political decision-making:

> And this is the reason, Socrates, why the Athenians, and man-
> kind in general, when the question relates to excellence in carpentry
> or any other mechanical art, allow but a few to share in their deliber-
> ations. And when anyone else interferes, then as you say, they object
> if he be not of the few; which, as I reply, is very natural. But when
> they meet to deliberate about political excellence or virtue, which
> proceeds only by way of justice and self-control, they are patient
> enough of any man who speaks of them, as is also natural, because
> they think that every man ought to share in this sort of virtue, and
> that states could not exist if this were otherwise. (¶322d–323a)

The "ought" construction is significant here. Even though everyone "ought" to be able to participate, the Athenians, says Protagoras,
"do not conceive this virtue to be given by nature, or to grow
spontaneously, but to be a thing which is taught, and which comes
to a man by taking pains" (¶323c–d). Though the principle skill of
the democracy is rhetoric, Protagoras does not concentrate on it in
his description of the ideal education. Indeed, his curriculum includes
a broad range of subjects, including literature, music, and physical
training, as against the specialization on which Plato insists in the
Republic. While the sophists concentrated on rhetoric, political science, and debate, their curriculum did entertain questions about
physical science (Kerferd 39), as well as literary performance and
criticism. Protagoras advocates "a holistic view of discourse that did
not distinguish between the aesthetic and functional" (Barrett 39).

What we see laid out in the "logos" of Protagoras's "Great
Speech" is a program for a cultural education; we might call it an
ideological education in the values of the community, "commenc-
[ing] in the first years of childhood, and last[ing] to the very end of
life" (¶325c). The most prominent feature of his whole educational

scheme—the one that may stand out the most for us today—is the idea of punishment for those who fail to follow not only the laws but the manners of the polis. As the early teachers—mother, father, tutor—work with the child, they are constantly "setting forth to him that this is just and that is unjust; this is noble, that is base; this is pious, that is impious; do this and don't do that" (¶325d). Protagoras describes the life-long cultural process of education in the broadest sense through which the individual is shaped in the mold of the group. At the highest level, "the city draws the laws, which were the invention of good lawgivers living in the olden time, and compels the young man to rule and be ruled in accordance with them. He who transgresses them is to be corrected or, in other words, called to account, which is a term used not only in your country, but also in many others, seeing that justice calls men to account" (¶326d).

Described here is no less than a comprehensive process of socialization. Its presentation here—in references, for example to good lawgivers in the "olden time" (¶326d)—may make us wonder, however, how the sophistic education could provide the kind of critique of tradition, of ideology, necessary for change. Havelock draws attention to the critical value of simply bringing to light habitual, unconscious practices: "Sophistic sociology would then perform the historical service of discovering that there was such a thing as 'education,' which as handled within the family became an identifiable process though only part of the over-all mechanism by which society conserved itself" (*Temper* 180). Not only did the sophists bring to consciousness an unconscious process, but more significantly they deployed their contribution to it in association with democracy: "Democracy, with its egalitarian thrust and structural dependence on verbal persuasion in the assembly, was felt to be in harmony with the anthropological 'facts' of the human condition: the necessity for cooperation, mutual respect, and the substitution of persuasion for force. . . . The importance of persuasion and the general celebration of human intelligence in anthropology validated the primary activity of the 'sophist' in the narrowest sense of the term, i.e., teaching rhetoric and political science to those who aspired to power in the democracy" (Rose, "*Philoctetes*" 53–54).

To move from Protagoras's anthropological account of human origins and the possibility for teaching virtue to a commentary on the specifics of a rhetorical education requires positioning language practice in relation to social and political practice, and in the process redefines "technique." Whereas Jaeger read the third stage of the Protagorian creation myth as a happy transcendence of the "technical" (i.e. the stage of building houses, etc.), Havelock finds the techniques of language used by the sophists consistent with their anthropology: "Technique is generic to the human race" (*Temper* 192). Habits of language, acquired through social practice, become a form of social influence: "Discourse as a technique and political judgment as an operation of psyche go hand in hand. Each reflects our social conditioning and also helps to create it. Political judgment, indeed, is hardly distinguishable from communication. The effectiveness of one is also the effectiveness of the other" (Havelock, *Temper* 193). Ober as well defines political participation in the polis itself as an education in communal decision-making (159). From the time after the reforms of Cleisthenes, the practice of *isegoria* enabled any citizen to speak before the assembly, introducing proposals on which there would most often arise different opinions (Ober 78). This practice "changed the nature of mass experience of the Assembly from passive approval to actively listening and judging the merits of complex, competing arguments" (Ober 79). Not only was rhetoric a democratizing agent, democracy itself was an education in language use and political decision-making. This extension of sophistic education was available to *all* Athenian citizens through participation in the democracy, regardless of whether they had purchased sophistic instruction or spoke frequently in front of the assembly. The case for communication between mass and elite refutes Jaeger's contention that the sophistic education was only for the leaders. The political experience in fifth-century Athens for all citizens was an education in communal decision-making (Ober 159–61).

The philosophy of language implied by these historical accounts is endorsed by many progressive theorists in composition and rhetoric today as in other disciplines. Bowles and Gintis, for example, in *Democracy and Capitalism,* assert that ideas do not preexist their enactment in language, that discourse creates social groups through the bonds of language. Rejecting both an expressive theory of social action—positing that action merely reflects the interests of individual consciousness—and a translation theory of language as a conduit for public expression of consciousness, they argue instead for an "anthropomorphic conception of collective social practices" (160). The tools of discourse both constitute as well as facilitate social practices.

The sophists taken together theorize the way a politically oriented or outer-directed pedagogy relates to individual mental activity associated with language use and reception. Gorgias's *Encomium of Helen* begins with a question about motive and action: why did Helen go with Paris? The answer complicates what Bowles and Gintis refer to as an expressive theory of action by reference to the power of language. That is, a single simple motive cannot accurately be inferred from her actions themselves. Impressions made by language in the psyche have a physical effect, an effect on individual action. "Personal" issues of desire, love, passion, and ultimately intention are articulated with public questions of the implications of action on the communal good and the ways decisions about such actions come about. Part of the sophists' contribution is to offer speculations about the structure and function of language as a framework for articulating those two spheres.

This Janus-faced picture of sophistic language *techne,* looking inward and outward at the same time, provides a way of gauging the critical potential of sophistic rhetoric. Protagoras's teaching was based on antilogy (Marrou 51), a method of opposing one statement (logos) to another or drawing attention to such a contradiction in language or affairs (Kerferd 63). Gorgias's apagogic method of argument—the exploration of various alternative positions—likewise offers the opportunity to reflect on the contradictory nature of propositions (Barrett 16–17). Marrou provides perhaps the most cynical reading of this teaching method, separating it from "rhetoric," and describing it as a practice of "low cunning" that put tactical tricks on the same level as rational argument (52). Aristotle spoke scornfully of the practice in the *Rhetoric,* inferring its aim to be to "make the worse case better" (II.23.1402a23). But a reading informed by a democratic political agenda understands the process of discovering contradictory statements to be grounded in the sophistic belief that phenomena are characterized by constant change, and, further, that individual human perceptions are the only "measure" of phenomena. Plato allows Protagoras a more sympathetic and authentic explanation of antilogic as a language technique in service of democratic politics in his dialogue, *Theaetetus:* "Wise and good orators make what is beneficial rather than what is harmful appear just to the cities. For whatever sort of thing appears just and honorable to each city *is* so for that city for as long as it so deems. On the same principle the sophist too, capable as he is of educating in this way those under his instruction, is wise and worth a great deal of money as well to those he has taught" (¶166d).

What makes the practice of "antilogic" especially significant for an evaluation of sophistic education for democracy is its critical potential. The Protagorian account of the educational process emphasized the power of custom/law—of hegemony, in Gramscian terms— to dominate the student through all levels of education and to reproduce itself. By bringing the very process of acculturation to consciousness, "Protagoras" implies the possibility of a critical relation to that process—an ability to stand outside of and perhaps control aspects of it. But the technique of antilogic goes further, demonstrating how the sophist and his students actually engaged in a critical analysis of popular belief. Though some commentators follow Plato's critique in *Gorgias* of the rhetor as totally subservient to *doxa* (Ober 151), Plato himself provides evidence of the critical capacity of antilogic when he warns in the *Republic* against its misuse by young, inexperienced dialecticians; the result will be the destruction of respect for traditional authority (Kerferd 64). The paradox of Plato's warning inhabits the figure of Socrates—arch-critic of the unexamined opinion. But Socrates's dialectic, in the context of Platonic metaphysics, led completely away from the active world of the senses and of political work toward the higher world of permanent Truth.

For the sophists, on the other hand, the "technique" of antilogic is shown to be not merely a mechanical process of constructing contentless arguments but a natural outcome of sophistic epistemology with critical potential for engaging and shaping political thought and action in the polis. The same sort of case can be made for another sophistic pedagogical practice: the teaching of common topics. Memorizing lists of commonplaces, on a technical level, prepared the student to construct speeches that would be well received—i.e., easily recognizable—by the assembly or jury (Kennedy, *Rhetoric* 28–29). But on the level of ideology, cataloging and studying *topoi* brought forward for examination "the combination of beliefs and attitudes, often unformulated or subconscious and certainly neither coherent nor necessarily consistent, which underlay . . . thinking and . . . behaviour" (Finley, *Authority and Legitimacy*, 17; quoted in Ober 38). Because the *topoi* were themselves the contents of propositions structured by antilogic, sophistic teaching exposed those contradictions and inconsistencies in the matrix of accepted beliefs. It held them up for analysis and made them subject to choice. The values on which such choices were made, based on a particular vision of human history and desirable principles of social organization which we have preserved in *Protagoras* if nowhere else in the sophistic fragments, underlay sophistic "technique." In refutation of the view of rhetorical training in *topoi* that finds it totally in service of a set of fixed opinions held by the unreflective masses, Ober argues that rhetoric creates the capacity for a dialectical relationship between the leadership and the mass of citizens. This was particularly true in the formative years of Pericles's generalship. In fact, Pericles's responsiveness to public opinion was critical in shifting power away from a small, stable elite in fifth-century Athens (90–91).

Another *techne* providing a critical perspective on ideology is the practice of discursive exchange, as opposed to the set speeches most often associated with rhetoric. In *Protagoras*, Socrates himself admits the multiple forms of discourse at which the sophist is adept. "Our friend Protagoras cannot only make a good long speech, as he has already shown, but when he is asked a question he can answer briefly; and when he asks he will wait and hear the answer" (¶329b). In his analysis of this passage, Havelock notes that the Greek verb *dialegesthai,* eventually used to name Platonic method, would have referred to a more dialogic process under the sophists. Two important differences between Platonic dialectic and sophistic "cross-talk" concern the status of the student interlocutor and the value of his response. The sophist "did not seek to place the pupil at an intellectual disadvantage as compared with the teacher," waiting instead to hear a response which the teacher would take into serious consideration toward the outcome of the discussion (Havelock, *Temper* 212). The fact that Thucydides uses the verb in question to describe the negotiation of political disputes suggests that the method goes beyond a simple matter of conversation, becoming rather an educational practice in developing the skills essential for group decision-making and conflict resolution in a democratic context.

In setting apart Platonic and sophistic views toward language and justice, Havelock explains the inextricability of sophistic "rhetoric" from democratic social practices. He is worth quoting at length on this relationship:

> In the eyes of sophistic, man's morals are his *mores;* justice and law are inherent in the historical process and yet help to create it. They are formal names identifying patterns of act or attitude which may be still undergoing historical development. As names, they are modes in which man articulates his speech. As this articulation develops into increasing communication, so does the effectiveness of social organization and hence of moral and political judgment. Therefore there cannot be any question of going outside current discourse to discover the language of justice, nor of transcending current opinion in order to define its sources, any more than we can go outside the present city to discover an ideal state. Sophistic 'rhetoric' so-called should really be translated as the technique of linguistic expression. Sophistic argued that as this was studied and clarified and made more effective the norms of justice and social order became clearer. Moreover, discourse is social or it is nothing; its topics and problems are by definition common ones, group notions; the words of men act on other men and vice versa. There is exchange of opinion, alteration of opinion, discovery of common opinion, consensus and decision. It is not discourse carried on in the private soul. (*Temper* 193)

The sophistic education, then, in its theoretical grounds and discursive practices, promoted the democratic process of group decision-making on which our own democracy still rests. It remains to discover what traces of this ancient practice run through the teaching of writing in the North American universities of today.

Critical Pedagogy: A Contemporary Sophistic

Elements of the theory of language and society on which these sophistic practices are based undergird a number of contemporary composition theories. Labeled variously as epistemic rhetoric, social construction, or social cognition, these approaches to the teaching of writing share "an emphasis on the social nature of knowledge, locating language at the center of the formation of discourse communities" (Berlin, *Reality* 184). Berlin notes as well that even the composition theories centered on self-expression have been shifting in recent years toward social orientation (183–84). Because Berlin has provided full descriptions and analyses of such approaches in composition studies proper,[13] I would like to focus here on the most politically motivated pedagogical "school," one not yet widely engaged by a large number of composition teachers, in terms of its affinities with sophistic pedagogy and its promise for the profession. The critical pedagogy created by Paulo Freire and elaborated by North Americans Stanley Aronowitz and Henry Giroux and Ira Shor places the project of human emancipation—a liberatory democratic practice—at the center of the educational process. There are obviously great differences between training a small number of people for direct participation in a new democracy and these twentieth-century projects, particularly the North American situation of awakening a large number of people to the potential for participation in a heavily administrative, virtually moribund democratic system. But in their attempts at reinstating the public intellectual, conceiving of schools in Deweyan terms as laboratories for democracy, and empowering of students by giving them a voice, critical pedagogues revive the goals of the first sophists. In drawing parallels between these two distant educational projects, I hope to make the best case for the political pedagogy of the sophists and to endorse what I see as the most promising basis for composition pedagogy today among the options currently in circulation.

One feature of critical pedagogy resonant with the achievement of sophists is the emphasis on rationality. For Freire, "conscienciza-tion" is the process his working-class peasant-students undergo in coming to an awareness of the causes of their oppression.[14] Over-whelmed by the daily struggle for existence, these workers, finds Freire, "perceive reality as dense, impenetrable, and enveloping" (95). The irrationality of the working class takes the form of a mythical attribution of cause and of an inability to engage in analysis. Shor identifies the same problem in the working-class New Yorkers he teaches, using like Freire (125) the Marxist concept of false conscious-ness to describe an immersion in a mass culture which conceals from individuals their participation in their own oppression: "It conditions people to police themselves by internalizing the ideas of the ruling elite" (*Teaching* 55).

Aronowitz and Giroux, while acknowledging the importance of critical consciousness, argue that false consciousness is not the best way to describe students' apparent unreflectiveness about large social and political forces controlling their lives. They are especially con-cerned about radical theorists who find any talk about action and reform other than a full-scale realignment of the asymmetrical struc-tures of the economy an acquiescence to false consciousness.[15] They argue instead for a view of ideology as struggle, wherein humans reflect upon the ways they both reproduce and produce culture through their institutions and exercise agency to act in resistance to dominant cultural codes (32).

Though they differ in their terminology, all the figures under consideration here see language teaching as the key strategy for devel-oping critical consciousness. Freire, teaching basic literacy, speaks of naming the world as an act of empowerment (76); Shor encourages his students to examine the clichés that guide their thoughts (*Teaching* 69–74); Aronowitz and Giroux see language learning as a means of distancing oneself from the process of social reproduction (65). These themes of naming, of working through common expressions (*topoi*) toward a critical reconception of their use, of distancing by making conscious an educational process, have all been developed above as cornerstones of the sophistic educational edifice.

The argument for demystification, for rationality, sounds like Plato's critique of oral poetry. Indeed, Freire sounds quite Socratic at moments, claiming to act as a mid-wife in the birth of consciousness (33), desiring to overthrow *doxa* in favor of *logos* (68), and openly declaring a loving attitude toward his students (77–79).[16] Having already made a case against an "oral" consciousness in pre-classical Greece (chapter 2), I need now to indicate how the admonitions of the critical pedagogues concerning rationality differ from Plato's banishment of the poets. What is meant when the advocates of critical pedagogy endorse "rationality," a standard shown in the previous chapter to carry sometimes oppressive gender identification? While the rationality of critical pedagogy engages in a critical analysis of cultural experiences (rock music, television, movies) similar in some ways to Greek oral poetry, it is quite different from Plato's or Aristotle's *logos*. A primary feature is the interactive practice through which it is developed. Shor describes the kind of reasoning through which false consciousness is challenged as "systemic," meaning grounded in explorations of history and social organization, "holistic and dynamic" (*Teaching* 60); the Platonic *logos,* like the Aristotelian, is static and ahistorical. For Freire, knowledge is always knowledge of the world of the students, developed out of the students' own experience and only "re-presented" to them in the form of problems posed by the teacher. It is never "delivered" through a dialectic master-minded in advance by the teacher: "Knowledge emerges only through invention and re-invention, through the restless, impatient, continuing, hopeful inquiry men pursue in the world, with the world, and with each other" (58). Freire takes pains to assure that he does not wish to identify himself as a member of an elite group knowing more than the students. Unlike Socrates, he insists that the students determine the starting points and "itinerary" of their inquiries. Unlike Socrates, who aims to demonstrate that the interlocutor really doesn't "know" something he thinks he knows, Freire aims to show the students that they really do know things about the world, though they had thought of themselves as ignorant (50). Aronowitz and Giroux seek to stem the "relentless growth of anti-intellectualism in American life," a product of traditional American antipathy to ideas as such and of the recent rise of "visual culture" (48). Coming to consciousness would counter students' "enslave[ment] to the concrete" by engagement in a critical analysis of mass audience culture (52), but always beginning with a validation of student experience, including aesthetic experience (53).

Indeed, this interest in identifying and affirming the ways mass culture creates sensual pleasure and expresses desires, rather than remaining totally within a critical opposition to it, recalls an element of sophistic work seemingly antithetical to the tasks of the democracy—developing the sensual effects of a poetic prose style. Building on their historical continuity with oral poetry, the sophists explored the play of language—its effects on the whole person. Their development of pleasurable poetic effects acknowledged the continuing presence of the body—subject of appeal in oral poetry—while in content investigating critically the way language worked in and on both body and mind. For the sophists, in gaining rationality the subject did not lose desire, as in a Platonic philosophy built on metaphysics.

One of the primary means by which critical pedagogues move students toward critical consciousness is the exposure of contradiction. Like the sophistic practice of antilogic, contradictions emerging out of cultural discourses are brought to a level of consciousness so that they can come under analysis. The aim is not resolution, but rather an awareness of the way culture, structuring thought and action, contains contradictory messages, some of which do not serve the best interests of those members who hold them. Speaking of the "counterlogic" of acts of resistance, Aronowitz and Giroux explain how contradictory propositions can ground actions against the grain of a hegemonic "rationality."

Contradictions emerge through dialogue, a practice central both to critical and, as we have seen, sophistic pedagogies. Proponents of critical pedagogy all decry the loss of opportunities for participation in democratic discourse in contemporary settings (though, of course, the situation for Freire's Brazilian students under a totalitarian regime is much more severe than for the North Americans). But despite the severe curtailment of democratic participation under late capitalism, they argue for a revitalization of democratic dialogue. The classroom is not the assembly or the law court of Athens. Of this they are all painfully aware and warn about too high expectations for the kinds of actual change possible in the classroom (Shor, *Teaching* xi). But they do not see the classroom as an ivory tower—a refuge from the "real" world. Rather they see it as one of the most significant sites for the practice of democracy. Shor, using a sophistic style also favored by Freire, finds that "The practice of democracy in study is the study of democracy in practice" (*Teaching* 96). Combatting the power of authority in social organizations of all types to inhibit democratic speech, Shor offers a range of techniques for reintroducing the practice of speaking and writing to students silenced by their experience of United States democracy. Aronowitz and Giroux describe the liberatory classroom as a democratic public sphere, now taking the place of older forums once available for speech and democratic action such as labor unions and churches. Redefining the "literacy crisis" as a problem of "conceptual illiteracy" rather than a matter of technical proficiency with language, they find students today "unable to examine critically public and private life . . . and to make public choices that become policy" (64). Their concept of "public sphere" bridges the distance between a small Athenian democracy and a huge industrial state as they find possibilities for democratic mediation in government action in many arenas of social life: church associations, trade unions, social movements, and others. Aronowitz and Giroux envision a form of "citizenship" like the *arete* Protagoras taught, a "form of political and ethical scrutiny that defines citizenship not as a function of the state but as a quality that permeates all of social life, a quality that speaks to forms of critical literacy and social empowerment aimed at developing democratic and just communities" (205).

The role of dialogue in the movement from "critical thinking" to action differs distinctly from the aim of Platonic dialectic—reaching stable Truth. The direction of dialogue in critical pedagogy resembles the future orientation of sophistic rhetoric. In its debt to Heraclitus, sophistic thought begins with the assumption that the physical world is in flux, and it builds its social theory and practice on that understanding. Both Poulakos's analysis of the sophists, set forth within a Hiedeggerian frame ("Possible") and Freire's Hegelian historicism envision the human as "becoming." An unreflective stance toward the self and world can be described as a fix in the moment: "For the naïve thinker, the important thing is accommodation to this normalized 'today.' For the critic, the important thing is the continuing transformation of reality, in behalf of the continuing humanization of men" (Freire 81). Aronowitz and Giroux repeatedly emphasize the importance of moving beyond a pessimistic critique of the inadequacies of today's education toward a language of hope and possibility for solving the political problems of the democracy. They define education as a process not only of socialization but of "assimilating the world to the dictates of the sphere we call 'imaginary' " (18). The impulse toward creating alternative worlds which Aronowitz and Giroux find in child's play appears, I would suggest, in the playful and future-directed "technologies" of sophistic rhetoric.

Feminist/Sophistic Composition Pedagogy

For pedagogies struggling directly with contradictions raised by gender and race—pedagogies in which conflict is central—I turn to the research of Kathleen Weiler and the radical black feminism of bell hooks. Weiler's work gives a feminist turn to the critical pedagogy of Freire, Giroux, and others. Her book, *Women Teaching for Change,* is particularly interesting for an articulation with the first sophists because it moves beyond the supportive context of personal experience in an examination of classroom discussions in which gender, race, and class create conflicts among students and teacher. Weiler grounds her study in an analysis of schools as places where culture is both reproduced and produced. Though the power and control of the existing social order is worked onto students through educational institutions, they are at the same time places where students and teachers can challenge, oppose, and resist those forces. Her project, then, given that potential, is to work toward "a more fully developed theory of gender in an examination of the lived experiences of teachers and students in schools" (24).

Weiler observed feminist high school teachers who taught a range of subjects including composition to students from a wide variety of class, race, and gender locations (130). Her description of these teachers' strengths develops the movement I would like to see in composition teaching in general. Like many composition teachers brought up on Elbow, Murray, and Macrorie, the teachers she observes "expand the limits of discourse by directly addressing the forces that shape their students' lives . . . attempt[ing] to legitimize their students' voices by acknowledging their students' own experiences and by calling for their students' own narratives" (131). But the teachers Weiler observes go further than creating a nurturing, student-centered classroom: "Related to the expansion of discourse, is their own presentation of themselves as gendered subjects with a personal perspective on issues of gender and race. They are overtly political in their presentation and both will use personal anecdotes and *will challenge and engage students on these topics*" (Weiler 131, emphasis added). In foregrounding their membership in a class, race, and gender, these teachers will either affirm *or conflict* with their students' own identities. They create a classroom in which personal experience is important material but openly acknowledge that differences exist and will create conflicts. The negotiation of those conflicts becomes the subject of the fragments of dialogue Weiler quotes and comments on. Not all the discussions Weiler relates show the teacher smoothly mediating conflicting positions of her students. In one example, a working-class girl, questioning the morality of the rape victim who left her children at home to go to a bar, is silenced by the middle-class feminist students (138). In another, the contribution of a black boy, wanting to read a segment of *The Autobiography of Malcolm X* in terms of racism, is passed over by his white teacher, who is making a point about socialization (140). The goal of Weiler's account is not merely to showcase exemplary teachers but rather to capture and analyze the highly complex collisions of gender, race, and class in the classroom. There is no sense of aiming to rid the classroom of conflict because it is "always a site of conflict, and will be a site of conflict for the feminist or critical teacher . . . just as much as it will be for a traditional or authoritarian teacher" (137). The recognition of this inevitability of conflict—in sophistic terms, a recognition of *dissoi logoi*—is not grounds for despair, but rather the starting point for creating a consciousness in students and teachers through which the inequalities generating those conflicts can be acknowledged and transformed (144–45).

The teacher's role in the writing classroom, on the lines of a feminist/sophistic pedagogy, would vary greatly depending on the make-up of the class in relation to his/her own subjectivity. Beyond recognizing her power *as* a teacher, she would recognize, for example, an unequal positioning if she were the product of a working-class background but teaching in an elite school. A black man teaching all white students would face a much different setting. In the polyphony of voices, not all will or should sound equally. Shor, using Freire, explains how the teacher, even while creating a "loving matrix" for dialogue (95) may sometimes need to take on an adversarial role against an abusive student, or to voice an unrepresented view in the dialogue (102).

An eloquent and powerful example of how, even among women, voices differ, bell hooks speaks directly to the issue of conflict in the title of her recent collection of essays, *Talking Back*. While the stereotype of women's speech under patriarchy is that it is silenced, hooks remembers women's voices as strong and angry in her experience as a child in a Southern black family and community. She was silenced not by men but by the adult women in her family trying to socialize her as a female child into using the right kind of speech (6). For black women, hooks explains, "our struggle has not been to emerge from silence into speech but to change the nature and direction of our speech, to make a speech that compels listeners, one that is heard" (6). Using her favorite teacher as a model, hooks endorses a pedagogy grounded in "an oppositional world view"—essential for blacks in a white racist society (49). Her teachers, almost all black women, "offered to us a legacy of liberatory pedagogy that demanded active resistance and rebellion against sexism and racism" (50). Hooks's analysis of the current educational climate grounds her pedagogical choices. Students today, she writes, "suffer from a crisis of meaning, unsure about what has value in life"; they "long for a context where their subjective needs can be integrated with study" (51). Hooks recommends a class wherein "the primary focus is a broader spectrum of ideas and modes of inquiry, in short a dialectical context where there is serious and rigorous critical exchange" (51). In this frank description, she describes a pedagogy similar perhaps to the agonistic practice of sophistic cross-talk:

> Unlike the stereotypical feminist model that suggests women best come to voice in an atmosphere of safety (one in which we are all going to be kind and nurturing), I encourage students to work at coming to voice in an atmosphere where they may be afraid or see themselves at risk. The goal is to enable all students, not just an assertive few, to feel empowered in a rigorous, critical discussion. Many students find this pedagogy difficult, frightening, and very demanding. They do not usually come away from my class talking about how much they enjoyed the experience. (53)

While this account may make advocates of a more supportive, non-confrontational writing class uneasy, commitment to a sophistic process of weighing contradictory opinions suggests that we may need to reassess the criteria by which we evaluate success in the writing class. The two pedagogies offered here as feminist/sophistic differ from other feminist work with writing—work emphasizing the nurturing role of the writing teacher. My concern about those feminist compositionists is that they may spend too little time helping their students learn how to argue about "public" issues—making the turn from the personal back out to the public (see Annas). As Gayatri Spivak has pointed out, a mere inversion of the public/private hierarchy succeeds only in dividing more rigidly two traditional realms. Just as "the so-called public sector is woven of the so-called private, the definition of the private is marked by a public potential, since it *is* the weave, or texture, of public activity" (*Worlds* 103, emphasis in original). My hopes are pinned on composition courses whose instructors help their students to locate personal experience in historical and social contexts—courses which lead students to see how differences emerging from their texts and discussions have more to do with those contexts than they do with an essential and unarguable individuality. I envision a composition course in which students argue about the ethical implications of discourse on a wide range of subjects and, in so doing, come to identify their personal interests with others, understand those interests as implicated in a larger social setting, and advance them in a public voice. Such a "content" for composition would replicate closely the sophist Protagoras's identification of the goals of the rhetoric he teaches: "prudence in affairs private as well as public; [through this course, the students will] learn to order their own houses in the best manner, and will be able to speak and act most powerfully in the affairs of the state" (*Protagoras* ¶318e–319a).

The alignment of rhetoric and feminism noted in the previous chapter emerges again in the pedagogies of Weiler and hooks. The discursive method driving both feminist and sophistic ways of negotiating change through discourse is argument, wherein rhetorical positions stand temporarily as grounds for action in the absence of universally verifiable truth. When we recognizing the need to confront the different truths our students bring to our classes—not only through self-discovery but in the heat of argument—feminism and rhetoric become allies in contention with the forces of oppression troubling us all.

Conclusion

This pedagogical overview has explored the essential interconnection of sophistic *technai*, or teaching techniques, with their theories of society, language and "reality." It establishes the sophists as public intellectuals with a political commitment but does not position them away from the realms of the private: neither from internal responses to language and reality, nor from issues of human relations on levels other than the city. In these ways, I feel the sophists made a valuable contribution to their own world and provide for us a desirable model for emulation in deciding questions about the relation of theory to practice and the relation of school to politics.

Though my goal in this final chapter has not been a wholesale reinstatement of sophistic rhetoric as a model for contemporary composition teaching, I do advance a reinterpretation of the history of classical rhetoric in order to forward the cause of a politically progressive composition pedagogy. Understanding that sophistic educational practice is inseparable from sophistic social theory and politics makes the point historically that *any* educational theory is "an eminently political discourse that emerges from and characterizes an expression of struggle over what forms of authority, orders of representation, forms of moral regulation, and versions of the past and future should be legitimated, passed on, and debated within specific pedagogical sites" (Aronowitz and Giroux 32). Of course, connections between education, social theory, and political program could be drawn for Plato and Aristotle as well. But what cannot be said about the fourth-century philosophers is that their pedagogy served the first and longest lasting direct democracy. For those composition teachers who wish to participate in the revitalization of our own democracy, the voice of sophistic rhetoric speaks out in playful, persuasive, and promising tones.

Notes

Works Cited

Index

NOTES

Introduction: Redefining Classical Rhetoric

1. Despite the absence of reference to the sophists in works like *Essays on Classical Rhetoric and Modern Discourse* (ed. Connors, Ede, and Lunsford) and *The Rhetorical Tradition and Modern Writing* (ed. Murphy), a number of scholars have begun a reconsideration of their contributions. These will be taken up in some detail in chapter 1.

2. The Greek texts appear in Diels and Kranz. Of the two English translations, Rosamond Kent Sprague's collection includes more complete versions of the materials than Kathleen Freeman's. References to Sprague throughout indicate page numbers.

3. Weaver and Stewart offer readings of Plato which essentially keep in place rhetoric subordinated to a transcendent value system. Covino and Golden argue for a more open and inquiring role for rhetoric in Plato.

4. The continuing centrality of Corbett's work, especially, for teachers of composition can be measured by its appearance as a central point of reference for history in works like Lindemann's *A Rhetoric for Writing Teachers* (34) and by its recent appearance in a third edition.

5. In the collection *Essays on Classical Rhetoric and Modern Discourse* (Connors, Ede, and Lunsford, eds.), the articles by Lunsford and Ede, D'Angelo, N. Johnson, Raymond, and Troyka focus on Aristotelian materials. Only D'Angelo makes more than a passing reference to the sophists.

6. In the later book, Kennedy grants that some sophists, "Protagoras, for example, may rightly be thought of as philosophers who developed ideas and published treatises on what we might call epistemology, anthropology, linguistics, and [other subjects]" (*Rhetoric* 25). But he goes no further with Protagoras's contributions, concentrating instead on Antiphon and Gorgias. Kennedy cites one scholar's current reassessment of Gorgias (Enos, "Epistemology"), but ultimately discredits it, judging that it "probably exaggerates [Gorgias's] intellectual sophistication and credits him with an uncharacteristic power of conceptualization" (*Rhetoric* 31).

7. The most exciting work I know of currently underway on Aristotle is Janet Atwill's argument for rhetoric as productive rather than practical knowledge and thus relevant for a post-humanist theory of discourse.

8. There is a good deal of debate about what might constitute an Aristotelian epistemology. For arguments against the compatibility of classical epistemology with contemporary writing instruction, see Halloran, S. Miller, and Knoblauch and Brannon. For a qualified endorsement of Aristotle, see Lunsford and Ede. See Gage and Atwill for rereadings of Aristotelian epistemology on two very different grounds.

I agree with postmodern feminists that practices need not be bound permanently by the grounding assumptions from which they originate (see chapter 3). My concern is that teachers and scholars in rhetoric and composition acknowledge and work through such grounding assumptions, even if they are ultimately jettisoned.

9. The term "epistemic shift" is drawn from Foucault's description of three major knowledge formations in Europe from the Renaissance to the nineteenth century (*Order*).

10. See LeFevre (10–32) on Plato and Enos ("Aristotle") on Aristotle. Other scholars, while not taking explicitly critical positions on the two patriarchs, offer rich and complex rereadings: e.g., Steinhoff and Swearingen ("*Eiron*") on Plato, N. Johnson ("*Pathos*") and Atwill on Aristotle.

11. Guthrie warns against lumping Plato and Aristotle together in their opposition to sophistic thought, but acknowledges that key elements of Aristotle's system—i.e., his teleological view of the world, his belief in the existence of permanent substances, and his division of knowledge into hierarchical categories—parallel Plato's (*Sophists* 53). These premises ground an anti-sophistic tradition.

12. I am extending here Derrida's assignment to "Platonism" a founding role in the Western philosophical tradition (*Dissemination* 76).

13. Though I recognize many contemporary "philosophies" have nothing to do with Plato and Aristotle, for simplicity, I will hereafter use the word "philosophy," as does IJsseling, to refer to that particular classical opposition to sophistic rhetoric.

1. The First Sophists: History and Historiography

1. Though some scholars are at pains to deny any such borrowing, there are good cases for Socratic questioning as deriving from or at least emerging out of the same tradition as sophistic techniques of argument (Aristophanes's *Clouds;* Guthrie, *Sophists* 177f.; Kerferd 33–34). In Aristotle, the whole conception of the orator as responsible negotiator of civic and legal deliberations can be seen as a legacy of the sophists. Eric Havelock (*Liberal Temper*) is

particularly adept at identifying the ways in which the two later figures reproduced but edited the sophists' naturalistic view of the human species to grant it explanatory power but bring it in line with their less democratic political programs and their essentialist metaphysics.

2. This is not to suggest that rhetoric has been dominated by philosophy in every historical period—quite the contrary. See IJsseling and Streuver. On the development of "literature" in the nineteenth century, see Williams (especially chapter 3), Horner (117–24), and Eagleton. On the debasement of rhetoric within the American university curriculum in favor of literary criticism, see Ried.

3. For a different and somewhat more detailed categorization of recent histories of the sophists, see my "The First Sophists and the Uses of History."

4. See also Neel on the interdependence of Derrida and Plato (203).

5. Making a less enthusiastic connection between deconstruction and the sophists, Wendell Harris demonstrates how Aristotelian thinking perseveres even in the face of poststructuralist challenges. Harris characterizes the French theory as derived from the sophists, who in his strictly attenuated version of them are born of Zeno: they are practitioners of paradox, experts of eristic, logical tricksters, wielders of "sophisms" ("Zeno" 560; "Ecological Criticism" 119). But Harris openly grounds his argument in Aristotelian logic, accepting without question Aristotle's appropriation of the sophistic practice of arguing from contingent propositions. His condemnation of the paradoxical sophists and their spawn, deconstruction, is conducted on a frankly analytic basis—backwards through the glass of Aristotelian logical categories. But what Harris offers in place as an alternative program of "ecological criticism" reads very nearly as an outline of a generally accepted set of sophistic features: arguments from probability, an informal method of reasoning, the essentially social nature of discourse contexts ("Ecological Criticism" 129).

6. For a bibliography of the speech communication version of epistemic rhetoric, see Earl Croasmun and Richard A. Cherwitz (n. 1). Particularly useful in offering a critical evaluation of the controversy is Michael C. Leff. See also Cherwitz and Hikins.

From the perspective of classical history, I find the choice of "epistemic" for this theory problematic. For Aristotle, rhetoric is concerned only with practical knowledge (though see Atwill on productive knowledge) and is excluded from the realm of *episteme*, the certain knowledge which constitutes scientific understanding. Thus, for a movement against an Aristotelian rhetoric to call itself "epistemic" in the loose sense of "knowledge-generating" betrays an insensitivity to historical sources of the term. I find Michel Foucault's revival of the term in *The Order of Things* (English translation, 1973) less problematic. Used to describe one of several sets of conditions constituting historical fields of knowledge, Foucault's coinage can be taken as a self-conscious, historical relativization of Aristotle's *episteme*—a single, timeless system derived by intuitive operation of the mind.

7. See *PRE/TEXT* 3–4 (1988) for a set of rhetorical commentaries on the philosophical foundations of Berthoff's work. The highly polemical and misguided characterization of "classical" rhetoric as empty formalism by Knoblauch and Brannon is embarrassing evidence of the extent to which composition studies are diminished by a poverty of historical understanding. Anyone who had studied the sophists would be struck immediately by the parallels between the pedagogy Knoblauch and Brannon advocate and a "classical rhetoric" including the first sophists. See Enos et al. for reviews criticizing Knoblauch and Brannon by Enos, S. Michael Halloran, Linda Roberts, and Richard L. Larson.

8. While Guthrie (*Sophists*) and Kerferd include sections on sophistic social theory, the orientation of both treatments is toward legitimizing the sophists on Platonic/Aristotelian grounds; whereas Havelock consciously works toward uncovering the extent to which our understanding of the sophists has been tainted by their famous successors. See also Rose, "Philoctetes," on the sophists' political education.

9. It is helpful to keep in mind that the sophists came on the scene almost simultaneously with the invention of history as a genre. Herodotus, the "father of history," may have read in Athens in 446 B.C. from his account of the Persian wars. See John Finley on the development of sophistic style in Thucydides.

10. Nancy S. Streuver's elaboration of the relation between sophistic rhetoric and history in the Italian humanists informs the following discussion. Another source for the connection between rhetoric and history is Havelock's association of Protagoras with one of three historical myths arising out of early Greek political thought (*Temper,* especially chapters I-IV).

11. See *PRE/TEXT* 8 (1987) for other definitions of revisionary history by Berlin, Schilb, and Vitanza. See also Berlin et al., "The Politics of Historiography."

12. The category "traditional" is neither exclusive (e.g., Howell's discussion of Locke in *Eighteenth-Century British Logic and Rhetoric*) nor pejorative but rather is used to describe a kind of historical practice—the rediscovery and preservation of pedagogical materials—arising in response to the needs of the field at a particular moment in its own history. North lumps all histories of classical rhetoric together as "first generation" attempts to recover and preserve (66–67). Though he outlines a more complex process of historical inquiry than practiced by those I have labeled traditional historians (71–90), North's own narrow delineation of "composition"—the institutional practice of writing instruction since 1800, especially in the United States (67)—

and his nationalistic suspicion of "rhetoric" as "alien" (65) reinscribes the boundaries I advise historians to violate.

13. References here are to fragment numbers in Sprague.

14. The crossing of boundaries in the selection of materials for history-writing, like other features of the historiography I propose, is characteristic of new historicism. But, as Judith Lowder Newton points out, "many of the assumptions and practices currently identified with 'new historicism' are intensely familiar," having informed a wide range of critical practices for years (152). Her aim is to show the debt of new historicism, as well as postmodernism, to feminist theory (153f.).

15. All of Gorgias's works are included in Sprague (ed.) Accepting the arguments of Havelock (*Temper* 157), Guthrie (*Sophists* 64 and 265–66), Kerferd (125), Dodds (198), and Kirk et al. (20), I take the "Great Speech" as an accurate reflection of the views of the historical Protagoras. See chapter 2 for more detailed biographical data on these two figures.

16. White employs literary categories as "modes of emplotment" in the analysis of various forms of historical composition (*Metahistory* 7–11).

17. See Berlin et al., "The Politics of Historiography" for a lively discussion of this issue. See North on interpretive bias and the need for confrontation in historical research in composition (81–90).

18. Aeschylus's *Prometheus Bound,* written during the stirrings of democratic sentiment in mid-fifth-century, contains a long description of human development along the same lines as Protagoras's and poses the strongest challenge to a divine *telos* as a grounds for autocracy, though Prometheus seems to be defeated by Zeus in the end. The two lost plays in the trilogy might have provided a more revolutionary challenge to the Hesiodic view of Prometheus.

19. Though White sees Darwinian historiography as rudely mechanistic ("Fictions of Factual Representation"), in line with his reputation for contributing to the materialistic determinism of late-nineteenth-century thought, Darwin's own text, *The Origin of Species,* reveals qualities of ambiguity, indeterminacy, and openness in the narrative form which demand a reconsideration of such a categorization.

20. Havelock associates changes in syntactic structures with evolution in thought (*Literate Revolution,* chapter 11, especially 246, 253, 256).

21. This interpretation extends but does not contradict Kennedy's description of Gorgias's technique as *apagogic,* meaning that the orator leads the listeners through a number of alternative solutions (*Art* 168–70).

22. Though Thucydides lived through and even participated in the Second Peloponnesian War, he is thought to have composed his history of it after the war was over and he was in exile.

23. Though the two most complete productions of Gorgias and Prota-

goras have been offered as a composite of sophistic historiography, both moments are realized within the works of Protagoras. His famous agnosticism, the man-as-measure doctrine, and the title *Contradictory Arguments* all suggest the critical impulse.

24. Fisher's work on narrative as argument incorporates an opposition between rationality and narrativity, though he keeps in place an essentially Aristotelian logic of coherence, consistency, and fidelity as criteria for evaluating narrative arguments.

25. The Jakobsonian distinction between the metaphoric and metonymic poles is a clear analog to the relation between hypotaxis and parataxis. What is particularly suggestive about Jakobson and Halle's original discussion of the terms is the observation that most metalanguage about symbol systems concerns the metaphoric mode, whereas metonymy "easily defies interpretation" (95). White's reduction of metonymy to a structure ruled by deterministic causality (*Metahistory* 35–36) misses the complexity of the metonymic and the depth of difference between the two registers.

26. This formulation fits White's definition of emplotment by Comedy—"the temporary triumph of man over his world by the prospect of occasional *reconciliations* of forces at play in the social and natural worlds" [emphasis in original]—but not his view of tragedy as law-governed (*Metahistory* 9). Untersteiner's understanding of Gorgian epistemology is the source for my use of the tragic (140f.).

27. Among rhetorical historians today, Vitanza makes the most striking and successful attempt to use the antithetical style of the first sophists to achieve "tragic" dissolution, but he defines the "comic" in terms of parody rather than reconciliation or reconstruction ("Critical Sub/Versions").

28. Fisher advances narrative argument as a theory which seeks to account for how people come to adopt the *stories* that guide their behavior.

29. In its political interest, this "aesthetic" history differs from White's interpretation of Nietzsche's concept of myth (*Metahistory* 372). It follows Nietzsche in advocating dialectical movement between forms, different styles of historiography for various historical needs ("Uses" 72), and the value of history in the service of life (116).

2. Between *Mythos* and *Logos*

1. The lively debate over the "Great Divide" theory of orality and literacy and its implications for composition and rhetoric is summarized and extended in a recent edition of *PRE/TEXT* guest edited by C. Jan Swearingen (7, 1986). See especially Daniell for an attack on the orality/literacy split and Swearingen for a gradualist view of linguistic and cognitive change ("Literate"). Goody

argues against his inclusion in the "Great Divide" school on the grounds that he uses orality and literacy only as variables for description (41).

2. Ong, whose major interest is rhetoric, takes it as a primarily oral phenomenon, though he acknowledges the necessity of writing for the process of formalizing rhetoric as an "art" (108–112). He views rhetorical argument as an agonistic exchange of commonplaces: "formulaic or otherwise fixed materials inherited from the past" (111). Thus Ong connects rhetoric with the persistence of an oral consciousness, as does Connors. Havelock's divided mind on the sophists led to a whole book concerned with their political theories (*Temper*) but an almost total avoidance of them in his extensive literacy work. Among the other classical scholars, Dodds offers the most extensive and interesting view of the role of the sophists in the rise of rationalism. His work, along with others, will be examined closely in the section below on the sophists.

3. Homer, living probably in the eighth century B.C., wrote about a culture of which no one in his era had living memory, the warrior culture of Mycenae ending in 1200. The transitional periods are divided into the Dark Ages after the fall of Troy and the destruction of Mycenae (from 1200 to 900) and the Archaic period (through the end of the sixth century). Though the Mycenaeans had access to a form of writing (Linear B), they used it apparently only for accounting records. Its use is not recorded after the fall. The Greek adaptation of the Phoenician syllabary into an alphabet (one sign for one sound) occurred by mid-eighth century B.C. (Havelock, *Revolution* 63) and made possible the inscription and preservation of oral "texts" such as Homer's. Havelock argues that "full literacy" was not achieved in Greece until the last third of the fifth century (*Revolution* 185–207), though many scholars place the date earlier (e.g., Marrou 42–43).

4. I choose the masculine pronoun here and elsewhere in cases where the evidence suggests very little possibility that women ever functioned in these roles.

5. The appearance of rhapsodes in place of *aoidoi* (story-tellers) in the sixth century seems to suggest the beginnings of such a division. They were seen by some as uninventive mouthpieces for static forms of Homeric verse, though again this judgment may be the result of Platonic censure (e.g., *Ion*). Enos suggests their main purpose may have been preservation of Homeric pronunciation before and during the recording of the poems in writing ("Rhapsode"). They did offer interpretations of the poems as well, however.

6. Plato's own strategic uses of narrative seem to contradict his desire to establish the logical process of dialectic as the only method for achieving certain knowledge. Edelstein finds myth in service of rational argument. See also Friedlander.

7. Investigating the continuity of this concept from the Homeric period

into the fifth century seems to me a more productive historical approach than dividing off a "primary" rhetoric from its later "secondary" formulations (Kennedy, *Rhetoric*). For a critique of Kennedy on this issue, see Enos and Ackerman.

8. Snell acknowledges that the mythic paradigm "allows a more comprehensive glimpse into human behavior," but denies any capacity for change attending its appearance. It always functions, in Snell's view, to keep in place "a tolerable degree of certainty and stability" (205).

9. Of course, there has been underway for decades the project of establishing the "logic" of narrative through structuralist anthropology and literary theory (see for example Lévi-Strauss and Propp). The most extensive effort toward this end in communication is the work of Walter Fisher.

10. Kirk, Raven, and Schofield is the standard reference work for the Presocratic philosophers.

11. "Broad access" must be understood in the context of the very limited literacy of the sixth century. I mean by the phrase outside the confines of palace or temple, sources of pronouncements about law of all kinds in earlier times.

12. See Enos's convincing case for Empedocles's contribution to Gorgian epistemology ("Epistemology").

13. Solmsen offers a careful examination of contradictory arguments under the Latin name *in utramque partem disputare*. His analysis is particularly useful in its treatment of argument and persuasion in the tragedies (10–65).

14. Though Plato often purposely misrepresents the historical figures used as models for characters in his dialogues, Kirk and Raven, among others, believe the views attributed to Protagoras by Plato in this case to be "very likely original" (411 n. 1).

15. See chapter 1 for a summary of the narrative and n. 15 for a defense of Plato's character as a reliable representation of the historical sophist.

16. In his introduction to *Protagoras*, Vlastos outlines shortcomings in Socrates's attack on Protagoras and defends the sophist's strong moral position in the dialogue.

17. Poulakos proposes that the Helen of Gorgias's encomium serves as an allegorical figure for rhetoric itself ("*Helen*").

3. The First Sophists and Feminism: Discourses of the "Other"

1. On women in antiquity, see Pomeroy and Fantham. Though the sophists at certain moments in history exercised some power in Athens and her colonies, their advancement of democracy by teaching rhetoric posed a threat to members of the aristocracy eager to undo democratic reforms and return to oligarchic or monarchic government. Thus they were always at

some risk. Protagoras, for example, was exiled from Athens for his atheism, according to Diogenes Laertius, who reported that all copies of his books were collected and burned in the marketplace (Sprague 4–6).

2. This is not to say that Aristotle held the same views of women themselves as did Plato. In fact, Aristotle defines them as inferior to men and not worthy of being citizens (*Politics* 68).

3. Cixous intends, of course, for the word "man" to carry gender specification.

4. Her historicization of Freudian psychoanalytic definitions of gender, however, complicates any simple male/female hierarchy by tracing historical changes in representations of women in ancient Greece.

5. But duBois notes that it is only through "misreadings of Platonism, the literal, antirhetorical interpretations of the role of the philosopher, that Western culture rationalizes a system of binary opposition in which women are defined as not-A to the masculine A, or as A-minus-one to their A" (28–29). Jan Swearingen has been helpful in encouraging me to read the rhetorical as well as the philosophical Plato.

6. John Poulakos suggests an analogy between Helen and rhetoric but interprets Helen as a specific mythical character rather than as a metaphor for "woman" or a representative of all women (*"Helen"*).

7. Kristina Straub offers a provocative analysis and demonstration of the uses of style and fashion in recent encounters between feminism and postmodernism.

8. But see de Lauretis (*"Essence"*) for a sensitive critique of typologies of feminist theories, especially on the complaints against essentialism.

9. For a more detailed discussion of the rhetorical nature of feminist theories of subjectivity, see Jarratt and Reynolds.

10. Most historians place the sophists on a continuum of "progress" in the development of logic, moving from a poetic structure of Homeric narrative through the speculations of the Presocratics, gaining impetus from Plato's dialectic, and culminating in Aristotle's *Organon*. See Lloyd (*Polarity*) and Dodds. For an alternative reading of this sequence, see chapter 2.

11. I wish to thank Peter W. Rose for pointing out this omission in Protagoras's version of the myth.

12. DuBois locates the tradition of dualistic logic historically by positing a "pre-Platonic logic . . . not based on absence and deprivation or on estrangement from the divine One" (24).

4. Sophistic Pedagogy, Then and Now

1. On sophistic education see Guthrie, *Sophists* 41–44; Kerferd 30–41; Marrou 46–60; Kennedy, *Rhetoric* 18–21, 25–40; Barrett 4–6,36–40.

2. See Guthrie on the abundant references in Plato to sophists' taking money for teaching (*Sophists* 35–36).

3. But Berlin points out the political limitations of pedagogies centered on a private inner world of personal experience (145–55). Aronowitz and Giroux likewise note the difference between a sixties pedagogy of "relevance" and a more socially oriented education aimed toward democratic participation (133). I have outlined gender-related problems with expressive pedagogy in "Feminism and Composition: The Case for Conflict."

4. The topic of the Convention for College Composition and Communication in 1988, for example, reveals this continuing interest: "Empowering Students in an Interdependent World." The transcript of the first meeting (1988) of the Research Network, a national collective of researchers in composition and rhetoric, is full of references to "empowerment." See *Rhetoric Review* 8 (1989). Aronowitz and Giroux, however, see the split of composition from literature as a "sign of its technicization" and warn against the "tendency to degrade writing to its functional boundaries" (52). This issue vis-a-vis the sophists will be taken up below under "Technical Education."

5. Elbow refers to Socrates eleven times in *Embracing Contraries*. Endorsing the dependency of the student on the teacher as role model, he explicitly outlines the erotic dimensions of the association with a powerful teacher much as they appear implicitly in *Phaedrus* (96–97). See Stanger for a discussion of gender implications in the erotic dynamics of the one-on-one writing conference.

6. Berlin alternates gendered pronouns, thus his choice of "himself" in this passage is not exclusive.

7. The reason for using Pericles as a referent for the civic subject rather than Aristotle's definition of man as the "polis animal" is that Aristotle bases the freedom to engage in political life on the absence of necessity: i.e., he divides the household from the state, ordering slaves and women to take care of the physical necessities, freeing men to spend their time with public affairs. Plato located the political subject by means of his or her narrowly circumscribed contribution to the social order. The sophists, on the other hand, endorsed a fully social and political identity, though they began to explore how language and society shaped an internal mental landscape.

8. Distinguishing the "early" sophists to whom Marrou refers here (i.e., Gorgias, Protagoras, Prodicus, Hippias, and Antiphon) from others is most important in discussions about technique. The practices of later generations of sophists (some not even a whole generation from their "elders"), though traceable to the innovations of their predecessors, lost theoretical and political grounding and became the basis for much of the criticism that has accrued to the name "sophist" since the fifth century. The group Marrou calls the "lesser Socratics" (60–63), for example, are those "sophists" Isocrates singles

out for condemnation at the beginning of *Antidosis*. I speak here of the practices developed by that smaller, older group during the middle and later decades of the fifth century.

9. Kennedy classifies Corax and Tisias, earliest predecessors of the sophists, as technical rhetoricians (*Rhetoric* 19, 29); see also Lentz, 113.

10. See chapter 1 and also Richard Rorty, *Philosophy and the Mirror of Nature*.

11. Rory Ong helped me to see how the character "Protagoras" often locates Athenian practices in relation to those of other cities.

12. While the sophists are responsible for introducing an intensive higher education in rhetoric, see chapter 2 for an argument that rhetoric was a part of the aristocratic training from the Dark Ages forward.

13. See *Rhetoric and Reality* (165–89) and "Rhetoric and Ideology in the Writing Class."

14. Though the critical pedagogue's interest in rationality shares some elements with Jaeger's attention to "consciousness," there are substantial differences in emphasis and ends. These differences will be spelled out below.

15. See also Bowles and Gintis (21).

16. Ann Berthoff, perhaps because of her disciplinary identification with philosophy, does not find the Socratic elements of Freirian pedagogy inconsistent with his liberatory pedagogy.

WORKS CITED

Alcoff, Linda. "Cultural Feminism Versus Post-Structuralism: The Identity Crisis in Feminist Theory." *Signs* 13 (1988): 405–36.

Annas, Pamela J. "Style as Politics: A Feminist Approach to the Teaching of Writing." *College English* 47 (1985): 360–71.

Aristotle. *"Art" of Rhetoric.* Trans. John Henry Freese. Loeb Classical Library. Cambridge: Harvard, 1982.

———. *The Metaphysics, Books I-IX.* Trans. Hugh Tredennick. Vol 1. Cambridge: Harvard U P, 1947.

———. *Nichomachean Ethics.* Trans. Martin Ostwald. Indianapolis: Bobbs-Merrill, 1962.

———. *Poetics.* Trans. Ingram Bywater. *The Rhetoric and the Poetics of Aristotle.* New York: Modern Library, 1984.

———. *The Politics.* Trans. T. A. Sinclair. Rev. ed. Middlesex: Penguin, 1981.

Aronowitz, Stanley, and Henry A. Giroux. *Education Under Siege: The Conservative, Liberal, and Radical Debate over Schooling.* South Hadley: Bergin & Garvey, 1985.

Atwill, Janet M. "Toward Posthumanist Rhetorics: Aristotle and Productive Knowledge." Paper. *Conference on College Composition and Communication.* Seattle. 16 March 1989.

Bacon, Francis. *The Advancement of Learning.* Ed. G. W. Kitchin. London: J. M. Dent & Sons, 1973.

✓ Barrett, Harold. *The Sophists: Rhetoric, Democracy, and Plato's Idea of Sophistry.* Novato: Chandler & Sharp, 1987.

Bartholomae, David. "Inventing the University." *Perspectives on Literacy.* Ed. Eugene R. Kintgen, Barry M. Kroll, and Mike Rose. Carbondale: Southern Illinois UP, 1988.

Bazerman, Charles. *Shaping Written Knowledge: The Genre and Activity of the Experimental Article in Science.* Madison: U Wisconsin P, 1988.

Belenky, Mary Field, Blythe McVicker Clinchy, Nancy Rule Goldberger, and Jill Mattuck Tarule. *Women's Ways of Knowing: The Development of Self, Voice, and Mind.* New York: Basic Books, 1986.

Berlin, James A. "Rhetoric and Ideology in the Writing Class." *College English* 50 (1988): 477–94.

———. *Rhetoric and Reality. Writing Instruction in American Colleges: 1900–1985.* Carbondale: Southern Illinois UP/NCTE, 1987.

———. *Writing Instruction in Nineteenth-Century America.* Carbondale: Southern Illinois UP/NCTE, 1984.

———, et al. "The Politics of Historiography." *Rhetoric Review* 7 (1988): 5–49.

Berthoff, Ann E. *The Making of Meaning. Metaphors, Models, and Maxims for Writing Teachers.* Upper Montclair: Boynton/Cook, 1981.

Bizzell, Patricia. "Cognition, Convention, and Certainty: What We Need to Know about Writing." *PRE/TEXT* 3 (1982): 213–44.

———. "Beyond Anti-Foundationalism to Rhetorical Authority: Problems Defining 'Cultural Literacy.' " *College English.* 52 (1990): 661–75.

———, and Bruce Herzberg, eds. *The Rhetorical Tradition: Readings from Classical Times to the Present.* Boston: Bedford Books of St. Martin's Press, 1990.

Blair, Carole. "Nietzsche's Lecture Notes on Rhetoric: A Translation." *Philosophy and Rhetoric* 16 (1983): 94–129.

√ Bowersock, G. W. *Greek Sophists in the Roman Empire.* Oxford: Clarendon P, 1969.

Bowles, Samuel, and Herbert Gintis. *Democracy and Capitalism. Property, Community, and the Contradictions of Modern Social Thought.* New York: Basic Books, 1986.

Bruffee, Kenneth A. "Collaborative Learning and the 'Conversation of Mankind.' " *College English* 46 (1984): 635–52.

Brummett, Barry. "Some Implications of 'Process' or 'Intersubjectivity': Postmodern Rhetoric." *Philosophy and Rhetoric* 9 (1976): 21–51.

Campbell, Joseph Angus. "The Polemical Mr. Darwin." *Quarterly Journal of Speech* 61 (1975): 375–90.

Cary, M. et al., eds. *The Oxford Classical Dictionary*. Oxford: Oxford UP, 1949.

Cherwitz, Richard A., and James W. Hikins. *Communication and Knowledge: An Investigation in Rhetorical Epistemology*. Columbia: U of South Carolina P, 1985.

Cixous, Hélène, and Catherine Clement. *The Newly Born Woman*. Trans. Betsy Wing. U of Minnesota P, 1986.

Cole, Thomas. *Democritus and the Sources of Greek Anthropology*. Chapel Hill: Western Reserve U, 1967.

Connors, Robert J. "Greek Rhetoric and the Transition from Orality." *Philosophy and Rhetoric* 19 (1986): 38–65.

———, Lisa S. Ede, and Andrea A. Lunsford, eds. *Essays on Classical Rhetoric and Modern Discourse*. Carbondale: Southern Illinois UP, 1984.

Corbett, Edward P. J. *Classical Rhetoric for the Modern Student*. 2nd ed. New York: Oxford, 1971.

Corcoran, Paul. *Political Language and Rhetoric*. Austin: U of Texas P, 1979.

Covino, William. *The Art of Wondering*. Portsmouth: Boynton/Cook, 1988.

Croasmun, Earl, and Richard A. Cherwitz. "Beyond Rhetorical Relativism." *Quarterly Journal of Speech* 68 (1982): n. 1.

Crowley, Sharon. "Of Gorgias and Grammatology." *College Composition and Communication* 30 (1979): 278–85.

———. "A Plea for the Revival of Sophistry." *Rhetoric Review* 7 (1989): 318–34.

Daly, Mary. *Gyn/Ecology: The Metaethics of Radical Feminism*. Boston: Beacon, 1978.

D'Angelo, Frank J. "The Evolution of the Analytic *Topoi*: A Speculative Inquiry." In Connors et al., *Essays*.

Daniell, Beth. "Against the Great Leap Theory of Literacy." *PRE/TEXT* 7 (1986): 181–93.

de Beauvoir, Simone. *The Second Sex*. Trans. H. M. Parshley. New York: Knopf, 1957.

de Lauretis, Teresa. "The Essence of the Triangle or, Taking the Risk of Essentialism Seriously: Feminist Theory in Italy, the U.S., and Britain." *Differences* 1.2 (1989): 3–37.

———. "Semiotics and Experience." *Alice Doesn't: Feminism, Semiotics, Cinema.* Bloomington: Indiana UP, 1984.

de Romilly, Jacqueline. *Magic and Rhetoric in Ancient Greece.* Cambridge: Harvard UP, 1974.

———. *A Short History of Greek Literature.* Trans. Lillian Doherty. Chicago: U of Chicago P, 1985.

Derrida, Jacques. *Dissemination.* Trans. Barbara Johnson. Chicago: U of Chicago P, 1981.

———. *Spurs: Nietzsche's Styles.* Trans. Barbara Harlow. Chicago: U Chicago P, 1978.

Diels, H., and W. Kranz. *Die Fragmente der Vorsokratiker.* 7th ed. 3 vols. Berlin: Weidmann, 1951–54.

Dodds, E. R. *The Greeks and the Irrational.* Boston: Beacon, 1957.

Donlan, Walter. "The Dark Age Chiefdoms and the Emergence of Public Argument." Speech Communication Association Convention. New Orleans, 5 November 1988.

duBois, Page. *Sowing the Body: Psychoanalysis and Ancient Representations of Women.* Chicago: U of Chicago P, 1988.

Eagleton, Terry. *Literary Theory: An Introduction.* Minneapolis: U of Minnesota P, 1983.

Edelstein, Ludwig. "The Function of Myth in Plato's Philosophy." *Journal of the History of Ideas* 10 (1949): 463–81.

Elbow, Peter. *Embracing Contraries: Explorations in Learning and Teaching.* New York: Oxford, 1986.

Elshtain, Jean Bethke. *Public Man, Private Woman: Women in Social and Political Thought.* Princeton: Princeton UP, 1981.

Enos, Richard Leo. "Aristotle, Empedocles, and the Notion of Rhetoric." *In Search of Justice: The Indiana Tradition in Speech Communication.* Ed. Richard J. Jensen and John C. Hammerback. Amsterdam: Rodopi, 1987.

———. "The Epistemology of Gorgias' Rhetoric: A Re-examination." *Southern Speech Communications Journal* 42 (1976): 35–51.

137

WORKS CITED

✓ ————. "The Hellenic Rhapsode." *Western Journal of Speech Communication* 42 (1978): 134–43.

————, and John Ackerman. "*Letteraturizzazione* and Hellenic Rhetoric: An Analysis for Research with Extensions." *Visions of Rhetoric: History, Theory, and Criticism*. Ed. Charles W. Kneupper. Arlington: Rhetoric Society of America, 1987.

————, et al. "Comments." *College Communication and Composition* 37 (1986): 502–06.

Fantham, Elaine. "Women in Antiquity: A Selective (and Subjective) Survey 1979–84." *Classical Views* 30 (1986): 1–24.

Fenik, Bernard. "Stylization and Variety: Four Monologues in the *Iliad*." *Homer: Tradition and Invention*. Ed. Bernard C. Fenik. Leiden: E. J. Brill, 1978.

Finley, John H., Jr. *Three Essays on Thucydides*. Cambridge: Harvard UP, 1967.

Finley, M. I. *The World of Odysseus*. Rev. ed. New York: Viking, 1977.

Finnegan, Ruth. *Oral Poetry: Its Nature, Significance and Social Context*. Cambridge: Cambridge UP, 1977.

Fisher, Walter R. *Human Communication as Narrative: Toward a Philosophy of Reason, Value, and Action*. Columbia: U of South Carolina, 1987.

Foucault, Michel. *The Archaeology of Knowledge and the Discourse on Language*. Trans. A. M. Sheridan Smith. New York: Pantheon, 1972.

————. *Discipline and Punish: The Birth of the Prison*. Trans. Alan Sheridan. New York: Pantheon, 1977.

————. *History of Sexuality: Vol. 1: An Introduction*. Trans. Robert Hurley. New York: Pantheon Books.

————. *Madness and Civilization: A History of Insanity in the Age of Reason*. Trans. Richard Howard. New York: Random House, 1965.

————. "Nietzsche, Genealogy, History." *Language, Counter-Memory, Practice*. Ed. and trans. Donald F. Bouchard. Ithaca: Cornell UP, 1977.

————. *The Order of Things: An Archaeology of the Human Sciences. A translation of Les Mots et les chose*. New York: Vintage, 1973.

Freeman, Kathleen. *Ancilla to the Presocratic Philosophers: A Complete Translation of the Fragments in Diels, Fragmente der Vorsokratiker.* Cambridge: Harvard UP, 1948.

Freire, Paulo. *Pedagogy of the Oppressed.* Trans. Myra Bergman Ramos. New York: Continuum, 1989.

Friedlander, Paul. *Plato: An Introduction.* Trans. Hans Meyerhoff. 2nd ed. Princeton: Princeton UP, 1969.

Gage, John T. "An Adequate Epistemology for Composition: Classical and Modern Perspectives." In Connors et al., *Essays.*

Golden, James L. "Plato Revisited: A Theory of Discourse for All Seasons." In Connors et al., *Essays.*

Goody, Jack. *The Domestication of the Savage Mind.* Cambridge: Cambridge UP, 1977.

Gorgias. See Sprague (ed.)

Gould, Stephen Jay. "Bushes and Ladders in Human Evolution." *Ever Since Darwin: Reflections in Natural History.* New York: Norton, 1977.

✓ Grote, George. *A History of Greece from the Earliest Period to the Close of the Generation Contemporary with Alexander the Great.* 4 vols. New York: William L. Allison, n.d.

Guthrie, W. K. C. "Flux and *Logos* in Heraclitus." *The Pre-Socratics: A Collection of Critical Essays.* Ed. Alexander P. D. Mourelatos. New York: Anchor Books, 1974.

———. *The Sophists.* Cambridge: Cambridge UP, 1971.

Halloran, S. Michael. "Tradition and Theory in Rhetoric." *Quarterly Journal of Speech* 62 (1976): 234–41.

Harkin, Patricia. "The Post-Disciplinary Politics of Lore." *Contending with Words: Composition and Rhetoric in a Postmodern Age.* New York: MLA, forthcoming.

———. "Reifying Writing: The Politics of Disciplines." Paper. Mid-West Modern Language Association Convention. Chicago, 6 November 1986.

Harris, Wendell V. "Contemporary Criticism and the Return of Zeno." *College English* 45 (1983): 559–69.

———. "Toward an Ecological Criticism: Contextual versus Unconditioned Literary Theory." *College English* 48 (1986): 116–31.

✓ Havelock, Eric A. *The Liberal Temper in Greek Politics*. New Haven: Yale UP, 1957.

———. *The Literate Revolution in Greece and Its Cultural Consequences*. Princeton: Princeton UP, 1982.

✓ ———. *Preface to Plato*. Cambridge: Harvard UP, 1963.

Hegel, Georg Wilhelm Friedrich. *Lectures on the History of Philosophy*. Trans. E. S. Haldane. 3 vols. London, 1892–96.

Holmes, Stephen Taylor. "Aristippus In and Out of Athens." *American Political Science Review* 73 (1979): 113–28.

hooks, bell. *Talking Back: Thinking Feminist, Thinking Black*. Boston: South End Press, 1989.

Horner, Winifred Bryan. "The Eighteenth Century." *The Present State of Scholarship in Contemporary Rhetoric*. Ed. Winifred Bryan Horner. Columbia: U of Missouri P, 1983.

Howell, Wilbur Samuel. *Eighteenth-Century British Logic and Rhetoric*. Princeton UP, 1971.

IJsseling, Samuel. *Rhetoric and Philosophy in Conflict*. The Hague: Mouton, 1963.

✓ Isocrates. *Against the Sophists*. Trans. George Norlin. *Isocrates*, vol. 2. Loeb Classical Library. Cambridge: Harvard UP, 1968.

———. *Antidosis*. Trans. George Norlin. *Isocrates*, vol. 2. Loeb Classical Library. Cambridge: Harvard UP, 1968.

———. *Helen*. Trans. Larue van Hook. *Isocrates*, vol. 3. Loeb Classical Library. Cambridge: Harvard UP, 1945.

Jacobus, Mary. "The Question of Language: Men of Maxims and *The Mill on the Floss*." *Writing and Sexual Difference*. Ed. Elizabeth Abel. Chicago: U Chicago P, 1982.

✓ Jaeger, Werner. *Paideia: The Ideals of Greek Culture*. Trans. from second German edition by Gilbert Highet. Vol. I. 2nd ed. New York: Oxford UP, 1945.

Jakobson, Roman, and Morris Halle. "Aphasia." *Fundamentals of Language*. 2nd ed. The Hague: Mouton, 1971.

Jarratt, Susan C. "Feminism and Composition: The Case for Conflict." *Contending with Words: Composition in a Postmodern Era*. Ed. Patricia Harkin and John Schilb. New York: Modern Language Association, forthcoming.

————. "The First Sophists and the Uses of History." *Rhetoric Review* 6 (1987): 166–78.

————, and Nedra Reynolds. "The Splitting Image: Contemporary Feminisms and the Ethics of *êthos*." *Ethos: New Essays in Rhetorical and Critical Theory.* Ed. James S. and Tita French Baumlin. Dallas: Southern Methodist UP, forthcoming.

Johnson, Barbara, trans. Introduction. *Dissemination.* By Jacques Derrida. Chicago: Chicago UP, 1981.

Johnson, Nan. "*Ethos* and the Aims of Rhetoric." In Connors et al., *Essays.*

————. "Reader-Response and the *Pathos* Principle." *Rhetoric Review* 6 (1988): 152–66.

✓Kennedy, George A. *The Art of Persuasion in Greece.* Princeton: Princeton UP, 1963.

————. *Classical Rhetoric and Its Christian and Secular Tradition from Ancient to Modern Times.* Chapel Hill: U of North Carolina P, 1980.

✓Kerferd, G. B. *The Sophistic Movement.* Cambridge: Cambridge UP, 1981.

Kinneavy, James L. "Restoring the Humanities: The Return of Rhetoric from Exile." *The Rhetorical Tradition and Modern Writing.* Ed. James J. Murphy. New York: Modern Language Association, 1982: 19–28.

————. *A Theory of Discourse.* Englewood Cliffs: Prentice, 1971.

Kirk, G. S., J. E. Raven, and M. Schofield. *The Presocratic Philosophers: A Critical History with a Selection of Texts.* 2nd ed. Cambridge: Cambridge UP, 1983.

Knoblauch, C. H., and Lil Brannon. *The Rhetorical Tradition and the Teaching of Writing.* Upper Montclair: Boynton/Cook, 1984.

Laclau, Ernesto, and Chantalle Mouffe. *Hegemony and Socialist Strategy.* London: Verso, 1985.

Lanham, Richard. "The 'Q' Question." *South Atlantic Quarterly* 87 (1988): 653–700.

————. *Style: An Anti-Textbook.* New Haven: Yale, 1974.

Lattimore, Richmond, trans. *The Iliad of Homer.* Chicago: U Chicago P, 1951.

LeFevre, Karen Burke. *Invention as a Social Act.* Carbondale: Southern Illinois UP, 1987.

Leff, Michael C. "In Search of Ariadne's Thread: A Review of the Recent

Literature on Rhetorical Theory." *Central States Speech Journal* 29 (1978): 73–91.

Lentricchia, Frank. *Criticism and Social Change.* Chicago UP, 1983.

Lentz, Tony M. *Orality and Literacy in Hellenic Greece.* Carbondale: Southern Illinois UP, 1989.

Lévi-Strauss, Claude. *Structural Anthropology.* Trans. Claire Jacobson and Brooke Grundfest Schoepf. New York: Anchor, 1967.

Lewes, George Henry. *The History of Philosophy from Thales to Comte.* 3rd. ed. London: Longmans, Green, and Co., 1967.

Lindemann, Erika. *A Rhetoric for Writing Teachers.* 2nd ed. New York: Oxford, 1987.

Lloyd, G. E. R. *Magic, Reason and Experience: Studies in the Origins and Development of Greek Science.* Cambridge UP, 1979.

————. *Polarity and Analogy: Two Types of Argumentation in Early Greek Thought.* Cambridge: Cambridge UP, 1966.

Lord, Albert B. *The Singer of Tales.* New York: Athenaeum, 1976.

Lunsford, Andrea A., and Lisa S. Ede. "On Distinctions between Classical and Modern Rhetoric." In Connors et al., *Essays.*

Marrou, H. I. *A History of Education in Antiquity.* Trans. George Lamb. Madison: U Wisconsin P, 1956.

Miller, Nancy K. "Arachnologies: The Woman, the Text, and the Critic." *Poetics of Gender.* New York: Columbia, 1986.

————. "Emphasis Added: Plots and Plausibilities in Women's Fiction." *PMLA* 96 (1986): 36–48.

Miller, Susan. *Rescuing the Subject: A Critical Introduction to Rhetoric and the Writer.* Carbondale: Southern Illinois UP, 1989.

Moi, Toril. "Feminism, Postmodernism, and Style." *Cultural Critique* (Spring 1988): 3–22.

Murphy, James J., ed. *The Rhetorical Tradition and Modern Writing.* New York: Modern Language Association, 1982.

————. *A Synoptic History of Classical Rhetoric.* Davis: Hermagoras P, 1983.

Murray, Donald M. *Write to Learn.* 2nd ed. New York: Holt, Rinehart and Winston, 1987.

Myers, Greg. "Reality, Consensus, and Reform in the Rhetoric of Composition Teaching." *College English* 48 (1986): 154–74.

Neel, Jasper. *Plato, Derrida, and Writing.* Carbondale: Southern Illinois UP, 1988.

Newton, Judith Lowder. "History as Usual? Feminism and the 'New Historicism.' " *The New Historicism.* Ed. H. Aram Veeser. New York: Routledge, 1989.

Nietzsche, Friedrich. "On Truth and Lies in a Nonmoral Sense." *Philosophy and Truth: Selections from Nietzsche's Notebooks of the Early 1870s.* Trans. and ed. Daniel Breazeale. New York: Humanities, 1979.

———. "On the Uses and Disadvantages of History for Life." *Untimely Meditations.* Trans. R. J. Hollingdale. Cambridge: Cambridge UP, 1983.

Nimis, Stephen A. "The Language of Achilles: Construction vs. Representation." *Classical World* 79 (1986): 217–25.

———. *Narrative Semiotics in the Epic Tradition: The Simile.* Bloomington: Indiana UP, 1987.

North, Stephen M. *The Making of Knowledge in Composition: Portrait of an Emerging Field.* Upper Montclair: Boynton/Cook, 1987.

Ober, Josiah. *Mass and Elite in Democratic Athens: Rhetoric, Ideology, and the Power of the People.* Princeton: Princeton UP, 1989.

Ohmann, Richard. *Politics of Letters.* Middletown: Wesleyan UP, 1987.

Ong, Walter. *Orality and Literacy: The Technologizing of the Word.* New York: Methuen, 1982.

Ostwald, Martin. *Nomos and the Beginnings of the Athenian Democracy.* Oxford: Oxford UP, 1969.

Parry, Milman. *The Making of Homeric Verse: The Collected Papers of Milman Parry.* Ed. Adam Parry. Oxford: Clarendon, 1971.

Peaden, Catherine. "Feminist Theories, Historiographies, and Histories of Rhetoric: The Role of Feminism in Historical Studies." *Rhetoric and Ideology: Compositions and Criticisms of Power.* Ed. Charles Kneupper. Arlington: Rhetoric Society of America, 1989.

Phelps, Louise Wetherbee. *Composition as a Human Science: Contributions to the Self-Understanding of a Discipline.* New York: Oxford, 1988.

———. "The Domain of Composition." *Rhetoric Review* 4 (1986): 182–95.

Plato. *Gorgias.* Trans. Walter Hamilton. Middlesex: Penguin, 1971.

————. *Phaedrus.* Trans. W. C. Helmbold and W. G. Rabinowitz. Indianapolis: Bobbs-Merrill, 1956.

————. *Protagoras.* Rev. of the Jowett translation by Martin Ostwald. Ed. Gregory Vlastos. Indianapolis: Bobbs-Merrill, 1956.

Pomeroy, Sarah B. *Goddesses, Whores, Wives, and Slaves: Women in Classical Antiquity.* New York: Schocken Books, 1975.

Poovey, Mary. "Deconstruction and Feminism." *Feminist Studies* 14 (1988): 51–56.

Poulakos, John. "Gorgias' *Encomium to Helen* and the Defense of Rhetoric." *Rhetorica* 1 (1983): 1–16.

————. "Rhetoric, the Sophists, and the Possible." *Communication Monographs* 51 (1984): 215–25.

————. "Toward a Sophistic Definition of Rhetoric." *Philosophy and Rhetoric* 16 (1983): 35–48.

Propp, Vladimir. *Theory and History of Folklore.* Trans. Ariadna Y. Martin and Richard P. Martin. Ed. Anatoly Liberman. Minneapolis: U of Minnesota P, 1984.

Raymond, James C. "Enthymemes, Examples, and Rhetorical Method." In Connors et al., *Essays.*

Ried, Ronald F. "The Boylston Professorship of Rhetoric and Oratory, 1806–1904: A Case Study in Changing Concepts of Rhetoric and Pedagogy." *Quarterly Journal of Speech* 45 (1959): 239–57.

Rorty, Richard. *Philosophy and the Mirror of Nature.* Princeton: Princeton UP, 1979.

Rose, Peter W. *Sons of Earth, Children of the Gods.* Cornell UP, forthcoming.

————. "Sophocles' *Philoctetes* and the Teachings of the Sophists." *Harvard Studies in Classical Philology* 79 (1975): 49–105.

————. "Thersites and the Plural Voices of Homer." *Arethusa* 21 (1988): 5–25.

Rosenmeyer, Thomas G. "Gorgias, Aeschylus, and *Apate.*" *American Journal of Philology* 76 (1955): 225–60.

Russo, Joseph, and Bennett Simon. "Homeric Psychology and the Oral Epic Tradition." *Journal of the History of Ideas* 29 (1969): 483–98.

Schilb, John. "The History of Rhetoric and the Rhetoric of History." *PRE/TEXT* 7 (1986): 11–34.

WORKS CITED

————. "When Bricolage Becomes Theory: The Hazards of Ignoring Ideology." Mid-West Modern Language Association Convention. Chicago, 6 November 1986.

Scott, Robert L. "On Viewing Rhetoric as Epistemic." *Central States Speech Journal* (1967): 9–17.

Segal, Charles P. "Gorgias and the Psychology of the *Logos*." *Harvard Studies in Classical Philology* 66 (1962): 99–155.

Serres, Michel. *Hermes: Literature, Science, Philosophy*. Ed. Josué V. Harari and David F. Bell. Baltimore: Johns Hopkins UP, 1982.

Shaughnessy, Mina P. *Errors and Expectations: A Guide for the Teacher of Basic Writing*. New York: Oxford UP, 1977.

Shor, Ira. *Critical Teaching and Everyday Life*. Boston: South End P, 1980.

————. *Culture Wars: School and Society in the Conservative Restoration, 1969–1984*. New York: Methuen, 1986.

Sidgwick, Henry. "The Sophists." *Journal of Philology* 4 (1872): 288.

Snell, Bruno. *The Discovery of Mind: The Greek Origins of European Thought*. Trans. T. G. Rosenmeyer. Cambridge: Harvard UP, 1953.

Solmsen, Friedrich. *Intellectual Experiments of the Greek Enlightenment*. Princeton: Princeton UP, 1975.

Spivak, Gayatri Chakravorty. "Displacement and the Discourse of Woman." *Displacement: Derrida and After*. Ed. Mark Krupnick. Bloomington: Indiana UP, 1983.

————. *In Other Worlds: Essays in Cultural Politics*. New York: Routledge, 1988.

Sprague, Rosamond Kent, ed. *The Older Sophists: A Complete Translation by Several Hands of the Fragments in* Die Fragmente der Vorsokratiker. Ed. Diels-Kranz and published by Weidmann Verlag. Columbia: U South Carolina P, 1972.

Stanger, Carol A. "The Sexual Politics of the One-to-One Tutorial Approach and Collaborative Learning." *Teaching Writing: Pedagogy, Gender, and Equity*. Ed. Cynthia L. Caywood and Gillian R. Overing. Albany: SUNY Press, 1987.

Steinhoff, Virginia N. "The *Phaedrus* Idyll as Ethical Play: The Platonic Stance." *The Rhetorical Tradition and Modern Writing*. Ed. James J. Murphy. New York: Modern Language Association, 1982.

Stephanson, Anders. "Interview with Cornell West." *Universal Abandon?: The Politics of Postmodernism*. Ed. Andrew Ross. Minneapolis: U of Minnesota P, 1988.

Stewart, Donald C. "The Continuing Relevance of Plato's *Phaedrus*." In Connors et al., *Essays*.

Straub, Kristina. "Feminist Politics and Postmodernist Style." *Works and Days* 11/12 (1988): 151–65.

Streuver, Nancy S. *The Language of History in the Renaissance: Rhetoric and Historical Consciousness in Florentine Humanism*. Princeton: Princeton UP, 1970.

Swearingen, C. Jan. "Literate Rhetors and Their Illiterate Audiences: The Orality of Early Literacy." *PRE/TEXT* 7 (1986): 145–62.

———. "The Rhetoric as *Eiron*: Plato's Defense of Dialogue." *PRE/TEXT* 3 (1982): 289–336.

Taylor, C. C. W., trans. *Protagoras*. By Plato. Oxford: Clarendon P, 1976.

Thucydides. *History of the Peloponnesian War*. Trans. Rex Warner. Middlesex: Penguin, 1954.

Trimbur, John. "Consensus and Difference in Collaborative Learning." *College English* 51 (1989): 602–16.

Troyka, Lynn Quitman. "Classical Rhetoric and the Basic Writer." In Connors et al., *Essays*.

Turner, Frederick M. *The Greek Heritage in Victorian Britain*. New Haven: Yale UP, 1984.

Untersteiner, Mario. *The Sophists*. Trans. Kathleen Freeman. Oxford: Basil Blackwell, 1954.

Vernant, Jean-Pierre. *The Origins of Greek Thought*. Ithaca: Cornell UP, 1982.

Vitanza, Victor J. "Critical Sub/Versions of the History of Philosophical Rhetoric." *Rhetoric Review* 6 (1987): 41–66.

Weaver, Richard M. "The *Phaedrus* and the Nature of Rhetoric." *The Ethics of Rhetoric*. South Bend: Gateway-Regnery, 1953.

Weiler, Kathleen. *Women Teaching for Change: Gender, Class and Power*. South Hadley: Bergin and Garvey, 1988.

Welch, Kathleen. *The Contemporary Reception of Classical Rhetoric: Appropriations of Ancient Discourse*. Hillsdale, NJ: Lawrence Erlbaum, 1990.

146

WORKS CITED

White, Hayden. "Fictions of Factual Representation." *Tropics of Discourse: Essays in Cultural Criticism*. Baltimore: Johns Hopkins UP, 1978.

————. *Metahistory: The Historical Imagination in Nineteenth-Century Europe*. Baltimore: Johns Hopkins UP, 1973.

Whitman, Cedric H. *Homer and the Heroic Tradition*. Cambridge: Harvard UP, 1958.

Willcock, M. M. "Mythological Paradeigma in the *Iliad*." *Classical Quarterly* 14 (1964): 141–54.

Williams, Raymond. *Marxism and Literature*. Oxford: Oxford UP, 1977.

Zeller, Eduard. *A History of Greek Philosophy from the Earliest Period to the Time of Socrates*. Trans. S. F. Alleyne. London: Longmans, Green, and Co., 1881.

Index

Susan C. Jarratt is an associate professor of English and the director of college composition at Miami University (Ohio). She studied the history of rhetoric at the University of Texas at Austin and now teaches courses in history, theory, writing, and women's studies. In addition to work on the classical period, she has published essays on rhetoric in Victorian England, feminism and composition, and historiography. Her current research concerns feminist pedagogy and representations of women's discursive practices in classical antiquity.